The Requisite Courage

Endorsements

Kris McGuigan extends a thoughtful and compelling invitation to personal growth, provides the necessary tools to support transformation, and offers a direct challenge to step into our best selves in *The Requisite Courage*. Kris reminds us that what we most yearn for, both personally and professionally, often resides on the other side of fear. Bravo to *The Requisite Courage* and to all those who leverage the insights from these pages in service of their fullest potential.

-Rick Simmons
Co-Founder & CEO, the telos institute and Co-Author of
Unleashed: Harnessing the Power of Liminal Space

Kris McGuigan's brilliance, care, and selfless leadership shine through as *The Requisite Courage* shows readers that your greatest opportunities are on the other side of your greatest fears. Kris codifies her personal experiences and those of the renowned, along with science, into an interactive roadmap, transferring conceptual understanding into daily practices that will guide you to that other side.

-James Rosseau, Sr.
Author of *Success on Your Own Terms* and
CEO of The Corelink Solution

The Requisite Courage captures Kris McGuigan's heart and her smarts in a fast-paced, practical, and beautifully written handbook for career-minded professionals seeking to build resilience in the face of doubt. Her personal stories and practical solutions offer a framework for anyone looking to capitalize on change and disruption to embrace authenticity and write the next chapter of their life story.

-Elisabeth Sanders-Park
America's 'Tough Career Transitions' Expert
and Co-Author of *No One is Unemployable*

Kris McGuigan has written an immensely valuable resource for career-minded professionals seeking to unleash their potential, realize their dreams, and live an authentic life. Combining inspirational stories with data-backed evidence and practical steps, the book takes readers on a journey from fear and doubt to clarity, confidence, and consistency in identifying, pursuing, and achieving career and life goals. I highly recommend it—both for individuals and for career coaches seeking new inspiration, tools, and frameworks to help their clients move toward career and life fulfillment.

-Louise Kursmark
Author of 20+ career books and Co-Founder of
Career Thought Leaders Consortium

The Requisite Courage provides a compelling map for how to transform our lives and inspire others to do the same. Through moving personal stories combined with research-backed insights, Kris McGuigan provides easy-to-follow practices to discover your unique purpose, choose courage over fear and realize your deepest dreams.

-Ellen Van Oosten, PhD
Co-Author of *Helping People Change: Coaching with Compassion for
Lifelong Learning and Growth*, Director of the Coaching Research Lab
and Faculty Director of Executive Education at Case Western Reserve
University's Weatherhead School of Management

Kris McGuigan has shown her talent for holding readers' attention! This book offers insight, inspiration, and introspection. The chapters on fear are especially enlightening. Even highly successful people face uncertainty, imposter syndrome, and fear of the unknown—whether they admit it or not. It's how we recognize and overcome the fear that counts. Elevating your leadership in the face of fear is just one example of the value you will find in 'studying' (yes studying) this book. Take time with it. Sit with it. Reflect on it. You will find *The Requisite Courage* a personal and professional self-development tool that lasts a lifetime.

-Valerie Sokolosky
President, Valerie and Company Leadership Firm & Host of
award-winning vlog cast *Doing it Right: The Stories that Make Us*

The Requisite Courage is about how to confront difficult changes in life and succeed while staying aligned with your authentic self. I highly recommend this book as it provides a roadmap for bravery when taking those big steps in life. This book provides a trove of scientific research with real-life experiences that support incredible personal and professional growth. Every reader will find relatable situations in this book!

-David Strukel, PhD
Director of Burton D. Morgan Center for
Integrated Entrepreneurship

Tackling change can be uncomfortable, stressful, and simply put, difficult. To inspire us to respond successfully to this challenge, Kris shares her own stories of personal and professional disruption and the lessons she learned for strengthening confidence and courage along the way. *The Requisite Courage* teaches us all to live with authenticity while building an internal and external support system that promotes resilience and recovery.

-Francoise Adan, MD
Chief Whole Health and Well-Being Officer of University Hospitals
Health System-Cleveland, Ohio

The Requisite Courage is an invaluable resource, successfully coaching readers through making life changes. In fact, the author's guidance and wisdom gave me the courage to leave a nearly 30-year career and pursue my dreams. Combining a coaching perspective with loads of research and practical tips, *The Requisite Courage* shines a light on the dark places of uncertainty. Anyone searching for a new path will find Kris's insight and authenticity life changing. I most certainly did.

-Danielle Serino
Emmy Award-winning Journalist

The Requisite Courage is a practical guide for those looking to lead with authenticity and audacity. Kris McGuigan presents clear, straightforward tactics for building confidence in the face of doubt. Based upon her own journey of self-discovery, she helps executives identify their values, find their purpose, and establish a success mindset.

-Ernie Pouttu
President & CEO of Harwick Standard

I can hardly begin to tell you how impactful I found *The Requisite Courage*. I have experienced years of change and challenges in my life and have learned many lessons along the way. The need for courage being the most important lesson. In a complex, rapidly changing business environment, leaders struggle to find the right resource to empower and equip team members. Kris does an amazing job of coaching leaders and team members alike to embrace the change and welcome it; to actually choose it versus becoming a victim of it. I walked away after reading this book feeling even more empowered to control my destiny.

-Sue Ann Naso
CEO of Staffing Solutions

the Requisite Courage

How to Make *Brave* Decisions in Business & Life

Kris McGuigan

NEW YORK

LONDON • NASHVILLE • MELBOURNE • VANCOUVER

the Requisite Courage

How to Make *Brave* Decisions in Business & Life

© 2022 Kris McGuigan

Published in New York, New York, by Morgan James Publishing. Morgan James is a trademark of Morgan James, LLC. www.MorganJamesPublishing.com

Proudly distributed by Ingram Publisher Services.

A **FREE** ebook edition is available for you or a friend with the purchase of this print book.

CLEARLY SIGN YOUR NAME ABOVE

Instructions to claim your free ebook edition:
1. Visit MorganJamesBOGO.com
2. Sign your name CLEARLY in the space above
3. Complete the form and submit a photo of this entire page
4. You or your friend can download the ebook to your preferred device

ISBN 9781631958878 paperback
ISBN 978161958885 ebook
Library of Congress Control Number:
2022931820

Cover Design by:
Megan Dillon
megan@creativeninjadesigns.com

Interior Design by:
Chris Treccani
www.3dogcreative.net

Cover photo by:
Prince David
unsplash.com

Morgan James is a proud partner of Habitat for Humanity Peninsula and Greater Williamsburg. Partners in building since 2006.

Get involved today! Visit MorganJamesPublishing.com/giving-back

To Rick
With you, I pledge to repair one small piece of the world.

Table of Contents

Foreword

I attended a speakers' conference in Fort Lauderdale shortly after starting my business. Four days in, I was surrounded by sunshine and highly successful business owners. I was intimidated and feeling a little outside of my own skin. That's when I met Shola. He was walking across the promenade during a session break and something inside me said I should call out to him. I had heard him volunteer the day before and knew he was someone I wanted to know. We had an extraordinary conversation. He was unbelievably kind. And in that moment, I didn't feel so alone. Years later, we reconnected over my desire to write this book. I indicated it might be easier to write about resumes or salary negotiations—stay in the safe zone. Shola didn't hesitate to tell me what I had to do: Be real. Show full vulnerability. Give people the requisite courage they need to live their lives to the fullest. "This is what you were meant to give the world."

〰〰〰

I'm scared about a lot of things.

As a father, I fear that I'm not doing enough for my daughters to ensure that they will grow into strong young women who are ready to face the challenges of a deeply polarized world. As a public speaker, I fear that I'll say the wrong thing on stage, and my misstep will haunt me on the internet for the rest of my days on earth. As a consultant, I fear that my clients will expose me as an impostor and that I'll lose my ability to support my family through my work. As a suicide survivor, I fear that the suffocating darkness that visited me 17 years ago will somehow find me again.

You get the idea. I'm scared about a lot of things. Aren't you scared, too? If you are anything like me, not only are your fears causing you to live a smaller life than you should, but your search to find practical strategies to overcome those fears led you to this book.

In your hands lies the answers that you have been looking for. Personally speaking, this book has not only changed how I live and lead—it is also the reason why I'm able to write the words that you're reading right now.

〰〰〰

When my dear friend Kris McGuigan told me that she was using her considerable talents to write a book called *The Requisite Courage*, I was more than intrigued—I needed to read it.

Then she dropped a bomb on me.

"Shola, I want you to write the foreword for my book."

While I immediately told her that I was honored by the kind offer, privately I was terrified. Yes, there is irony (or a clever joke) hidden in the fact that I lacked the requisite courage to write the foreword for her book of the same name. It was only after reading Kris's words that I found the courage I needed.

Confusing? Let me explain.

Yes, I'm scared about a lot of things. Yet, very few things paralyze me with fear as much as the idea of disappointing people who I care about. Foolishly, before writing one word of this foreword, I craved the certainty of finding the perfect words worthy of introducing you to the brilliance of Kris's work. Luckily, as you will learn in this book (among many other things), certainty is not a condition for courage.

Fearless authenticity is available to all of us right here, right now. The secret to living courageously is on the following pages.

〰〰

Through Kris's elite storytelling, highly practical exercises, piercing vulnerability, and deeply researched techniques, you will undoubtedly become more courageous. Whether you are contemplating having a difficult conversation with a loved one, moving to a new city, ending a toxic relationship, starting a new business, reaching out for help when you are in a dark place, or dismissing the pesky inner voice that unceasingly tries to convince you that you're not good enough, this book will provide you with the road map to expertly navigate your next courageous move.

One thing is for sure, there is a brave decision you are hoping to make and finding the requisite courage will get you there. The only question that remains is, will you take the first step to begin this life-enhancing work today?

As Kris loves to say, "It's never or now."

Choose wisely, my friend.

Shola Richards
Best-Selling Author of *Making Work Work* and *Go Together*

Preface

For the record, I prefer to tell stories in a bar. There is something about having a cold bottle of beer and the stench of bad decisions in the air that helps me get into the nitty-gritty details of life's daring moments. The volume is up just high enough to keenly focus on facial expressions, exposing an authentic reaction. There isn't time to craft a careful response around a high-top table when you are several drinks in.

But this is different. These are words on a page that you are reading in places I cannot be. There is no liquid courage coursing through my veins. Only my raw and real vulnerability laid out for all to see. The upside? I get to share stories of bringing forth bravery in the face of fear in the hopes of moving you to courage.

The downside? To face my biggest fear. To put my courage solution to the test. To step out from behind my carefully cultivated professional gal persona and have her stand side-by-side with that flawed and frail girl in the bar. To say something in a theoretical forest when there is no one present and wonder, "Will it ever be heard?"

Writing these pages without certainty they would ever be read, ironically, created a chance to test the theory. To prove my model worked. To shift my mindset (even in the darkest or most obstinate of days) from fear to fearless execution. And the call for courage keeps coming.

It's never or now.

Introduction

There I was, preaching to others to follow their passion. Do what they love. Find their purpose. Yet, there I was, returning to my safe little office each day to earn a paycheck.

Stepping away from the security of my established career and the identity that came with it was terrifying. I had spent years—nearly a decade—denying what I knew to be my truth. Finally, it was time to heed the universe's calling.

In 2015, for the umpteenth time in my life, I walked away from stability and welcomed disruption—this time to start my own business. I was ready to stand on the principle for which I had championed so many others for so long. I couldn't continue to implore all my colleagues and friends and family to unleash their potential and follow their passion when I refused to surrender, when I would give into the fear and return to that office again on Monday.

So, I hung my shingle. I began this incredible, harrowing entrepreneurial journey to guide so many others to do the same—to follow what I believed I was meant to bring to the world.

Every organism has one and only one central need in life, to fulfill its own potentialities.
—Rollo May

I had experienced enough failure in my personal life that I understood the value that could come from rejection and disarray. I was eerily excited about how much could be learned from burning the plan and starting over with the hope of stepping more into my authentic self. I walked into the all-too-familiar darkness trusting there would be light at the end of the tunnel. Things got messy and emotional and disastrous. There were days I didn't think that I was going to be able to do it. Days I didn't know if I could carry on. But here I am.

Is there something you have wanted to do for a long time?

A dream you've wanted to chase, a move you've wanted to make, a hunger you've wanted to feed?

Has the terror of exposing your real and raw self to the world stopped you?

Are financial concerns standing in your way? Is it the lack of certainty that has you paralyzed? The fear of inadequacy that's causing hesitation?

I want you to navigate your way through those murky waters. I want you to feel the pain and simultaneous power of fear, make the hard choice, and step courageously into your true self.

And I'm going to show you how.

Likely, if you're reading this book, you crave authenticity and want to hold strong to your mission. You desire to live with courage in a way that champions others to do the same. You long to conquer your fears.

Change can be gut-wrenching, more so than you predict. But intentional change can be the key to unlocking the cage to unleash your deepest potential.

Facing tragedy from an early age, I haphazardly learned to find the good in change and ride the wave of disruption. Death, divorce, career transitions, startups, reinvention. I often chose my change before it was chosen for me, but that did not make the journey less difficult and scary. Each passage required unprecedented levels of courage. I wish someone had given me a map of sorts to help navigate the dark spots. To shine a light on the self-actualization milestones along the way.

And so, I give you mine.

The Requisite Courage is a roadmap for finding professional and personal bravery in the things that matter most. It is a strategic plan that will define your desired outcome and include the major steps or milestones needed to reach it. It also serves as a communication tool, a high-level document that helps articulate strategic thinking—the why—behind both the goal and the plan for getting there. This book will pave the way to living in alignment with authenticity and audacity.

For over 20 years, I have worked closely with successful individuals from all walks of life. From small to big business leaders, the objective is always to guide them in unlocking their true potential. On the pages to come, I will reveal the science-based practices and field-tested tips to accelerated self-discovery, learning, confidence, and renewal to create long-lasting results. We will examine the inevitability of change and I will provide you with the courage solution to drive fearless execution.

You will gain clarity around who you are and what you want, identifying patterns in everyday behaviors to heighten awareness. You will attach conviction to your realized purpose to fuel your drive. Together, we will explore and embrace the elements of life that align with your value system and learn to let go of that which does not serve you. We will address different types of roadblocks you may be facing. You will understand how to identify and label your fears and apply real-time exercises to face them head on.

Most importantly, you will establish daily practices to build resilience and breed constancy in your life. You will master the lessons of progress over perfection and take small steps to spark big change. You will unearth the essential practice of self-care, aligning your environment and your entourage with your courageous self. You will learn to experiment with change and exercise personal grace.

Along the way, I'll tell you about my successes and failures and those of authors, inventors, entrepreneurs, and other notable people I admire. I will share some very real and raw narrative from my own life so that you may see how these concepts of courage came to bear. How I was able to apply the principles within this book to make sure that I was not only surviving, but thriving, through each and every one of those changes. I hope that the stories resonate with you and you connect to one or many of the various persons introduced. Yet, if you don't see yourself in one of their brave adventures, just know that you're writing your own.

The chapters ahead are about resiliency, leadership, inspiration, career wellness, and personal growth and development. They will walk you through the steps that you need to embrace change actively, consciously, and courageously.

I have carefully designed **Courage in Action** exercises after each section to guide you in applying key takeaways to your individual journey. I implore you to take advantage of this coursework and set aside adequate time for the suggested reflection. Download and digest the activities as often as you wish, implementing them to the various aspects of your life and moments of change now and in the future.

Today, more than any other time in our history, we require access to a quick, easy-to-follow, real-time application of how it is we can continue to face and embrace the change that is happening in our lives. This need rings true for the changes that come upon us, as well as those we initiate for ourselves.

What an incredible time to take advantage of and leverage all that you are. This is the moment to step into your full self and live with fearless authenticity.

Ready, Set, Courage!

It takes courage to grow up and become who you really are.

—E. E. Cummings

Part 1:

The Catalyst

Chapter 1

Change Is Inevitable

||||||||||||||||||||||

I have spent the better part of my career guiding people who are contemplating a change in course. I have seen my clients (and friends) walk through everything from carefully prepared, no-fail career moves to spontaneous, life-altering revelations that prompted them to uproot their family and move cross country.

If you're living life, you've experienced change. There are as many possible changes in a life as there are people on the planet. We can talk about the science and nuances of change for days on end. In fact, science diplomat and success strategist Dr. Vishwas Chavan says, "Only those who are able to adapt to changing scenarios will continue to survive and prosper. Success is directly proportional to the degree of positive adaptation to change."[1] For the moment, let's focus on these two primary forces of change—external and self.

External change is characterized by circumstances far outside our control. This type of change may happen because a small business collapses or a beloved family member is facing a serious health challenge. Think about global events or unexpected disasters. In these instances, we may feel powerless or hopeless.

A self-inflicted change, on the other hand, may come in the form of leaving a long-term relationship or switching careers. This type of change is often initiated by a quiet voice that yearns for something more or a nagging desire for greater effectiveness and authenticity. While outside circumstances may prompt your eventual action, this type of change is always a decision you make.

Both types of change can be accompanied by a range of emotions: apprehension, apathy, or complete shock. The path through disruption reads like a cryptic treasure map. There is mystery, uncertainty, mishaps, retracing steps, and an unforgettable journey. Let's take a closer look at how we can be thrust onto this wild path of change and disruption.

Involuntary disruption

Unwelcome change from outside forces can take the form of an external loss: a loved one, a job, a valued relationship. It may also manifest as an internal loss—that of an identity, sense of self, feeling of stability. Sometimes you alone feel the loss while other losses are shared by a community. For example, the twenty-first century has been plagued by continued social unrest, racial violence, and ethnic inequality. The macro issue often manifests in one or a series of massive disruptions. The emotional toll of these large-scale events may be experienced differently by every individual and also affect large communities of people at once.

One of this century's greatest disruptions was experienced by—and greatly affected—our global community. COVID-19, a serious respiratory disease caused by a novel coronavirus, was first documented in December 2019. By March of the following year, the World Health Organization had declared a worldwide pandemic. Suddenly, visiting a grocery store or inviting family over for dinner became a luxury no one could afford. A rising death toll and mounting family responsibilities caused an increase in mental health concerns. The burnout was widespread and long-lasting.

The pandemic created professional unrest. Boundaries between work and home were blurred. McKinsey & Company reported that as many as two million workers worldwide were contemplating downshifting their careers or leaving the workforce in the aftermath of COVID-19. Moreover, women (especially women of color) were laid off and furloughed at a higher rate than men, interrupting their careers and threatening their financial security.[2]

How did the COVID pandemic disrupt your life?

Did it cause difficult change?

Research as far back as the horrific Chernobyl nuclear accident in Ukraine and the more-recent devastation of Hurricane Katrina in New Orleans has shown that the mental health impact of disasters outlasts the physical impact, suggesting today's elevated mental health need will continue well beyond the coronavirus outbreak itself.[3] A May 2020 analysis projects that, based on the economic downturn and social isolation, additional deaths due to suicide and alcohol or drug misuse may occur by 2029.[4]

When unexpected and unwelcome change enters our lives, it can be crushing. Being ripped from the status quo and thrown into disarray is enough to make even the brightest outlook begin to deflate. Moreover, we are given minimal time to process the change and all the emotions and accountabilities that accompany this new direction. The need for conscious courage is pressing. While overwhelming, confusion around where to begin is normal.

There are ways to make these changes less disruptive, even if it's merely a change in perspective. Sure, that's easier said than done, but in the chapters that follow, I offer concrete strategies for shifting your mindset and navigating the unknown waters.

Voluntary disruption

Beyond external interruptions, we are often called to courage when disruption bubbles up from within. Feelings of restlessness, longing, and misalignment can spark self-catalyzed change: a twenty-something considering a move across the country to start a new life; a middle-aged man deciding to adopt a healthier lifestyle; a college student changing their major course of study; a weary wife filing for divorce.

Long before he became America's dog whisperer, Cesar Millan was working on an animal farm in Sinaloa, Mexico. At the age of 21, Millan fled Mexico (and all that he knew) and entered the United States hoping to find a better life. He spent months homeless in California before securing a job as a dog walker. In the years that followed, Millan found opportunities to showcase his natural talents and became the world's foremost dog trainer and behaviorist, eventually starring in his own television show on *National Geographic*.[5]

Have you ever stepped into the unknown to better your life?

Did it bring the desired outcome? If not, are you still on the journey?

Even when change is welcome, it can stimulate our stress response. According to Christopher Harvey, Head of Change Management at Tesco, "People don't tend to think about the impacts of change, because they think they're better at dealing with it than they actually are."[6]

Here again, we have the opportunity to manage our response to change and embrace the disruption. Just as with the unexpected types of change that we discussed earlier, we cannot always control what will happen next. We will, however, explore methodologies throughout the book to guide you in planning, executing, and sustaining positive change in your life.

~~~~

One of the most significant moments of self-catalyzed change in my own life came when I quit climbing the corporate ladder. I, myself, had something of a quarter-life crisis. I was three years out of undergrad, and I started to get antsy. I wasn't finding fulfillment in my work as a project manager and wanted more, but I couldn't articulate what I wanted "more" of.

After weeks of introspection—poring over my job history, whittling down long lists of accountabilities to those tasks I found energizing, soliciting honest feedback from friends and family members, conducting informational meetings with mentors—I suddenly stopped. The realization that I was the only twenty-five-year-old conducting a self-driven career assessment knocked me over the head. I became acutely aware that it hadn't been the pro-motions I landed over the years that had fueled my fire, but the process of climbing the ladder. It was the art of changing jobs—the strategy and execution of figuring out where to go next and then making it happen—that I loved the most. The career development journey itself had been most meaningful. Like a child addicted to a video game simulation, I thrived on conquering the obstacle and earning my way to the next level.

And there it was: I had found my calling.

Once I discovered that career development was my vocation, I pursued a coaching credential and threw up some flyers (actual paper flyers; this was before social media took off). I spread the word within my existing network and took on clients during lunch, skipped happy hour to take a call, and hustled on the weekends. I was enjoying the idea of owning a business and helping people, but I didn't have a desire to market myself outside of my circle. The potential rejection factor was far too high for my precious ego. Projects at my full-time job were mounting, and my then-husband and I were thinking of starting a family. I took a U-turn. I packed my dream into a neat little box and placed it up onto a shelf. The fear of failure was looming, and I was all too satisfied to remove that from my sights and focus on the aspects of life I felt assured of.

In the years that followed, life happened. I moved three times. I had two beautiful children and one ugly divorce. All the while, I was following the corporate carrot. I was repeatedly offered bigger jobs with better titles, ascending to the coveted corner office. Yet, something still seemed to be missing. I had achieved many of the professional goals I had set for myself, but I still wasn't finding fulfillment.

It wasn't that I didn't like my job, I simply didn't feel much of anything about the end game. The part I found most enjoyable was leading and developing my team. I was that boss who called front-line staff into my office and persuaded them to tell me what they really wanted to do for a living, then helped them develop a plan to get there. Staff members would book time on my calendar to review their resumes and discuss next-level options. Every one-on-one would start with, "How can I help you grow this week?" Great for morale, not so much for keeping turnover down.

I was spending spare moments at work prompting colleagues to find their purpose and follow it with all their heart. Meanwhile, I was spending spare moments at home contemplating how far I was from my own purpose and the fear I would face trying to switch paths. It was so much easier to maintain the status quo and not rock the boat, no matter how off-course I felt.

Finally, in what can only be described as a detour sponsored by the universe, a flood of serendipitous moments led me to a conversation that would change my life:

One spring afternoon, my friend Michelle and I were discussing the future. I surprised us both by stating a wistful dream out loud.

"I'm going to quit my job in September and restart my business."

Now, you should know two things here. One, I have always strived to surround myself with people smarter than me. And two, Michelle is one of the smartest, wisest, most risk-averse individuals I have ever known. I expected she, if anyone, would talk me out of this cockamamie plan. Instead, she asked why I was waiting until September.

"What will be different then?" she asked.

I looked down at my cherry wood desk fixed in the middle of a spacious corner office. Shocked into silence, I thought for a moment and realized the long runway was simply a loosely veiled strategy to give myself enough time to let fear overcome. More time to talk myself out of it.

"What if I fail?" I asked.

She looked at me with a confidence I strive for every single day and stated, "I've never seen you fail at anything you've put your mind to."

And just like that, the decision was made. I turned in my resignation later that afternoon.

When in doubt, choose change.
—Lily Leung

〰〰〰

In guiding others through change in my daily work, my reaction to the initial hesitation is a mix of empathy and curiosity. My heart feels for those who are struggling to make a choice and are afraid to take action. A lover of puzzles, I am inquisitive by nature and crave all the tiny details to piece the picture together. As someone who has experienced disruptive change myself, I feel a compulsion to gather the variables to parcel out all elements that are serving the greater cause and distinguish from those that are just distracting from the end game. But as a coach, I have learned to exercise self-restraint, posing only those questions that provide relevant information to the issue at hand. Requesting details that are not pertinent to the solution is a self-serving practice.

I ask questions like:

"What is stopping you from following your heart?"

"Who are you capable of becoming?"

"Why haven't you pursued this path in the past?"

"How can you step into your true self?"

And it never fails, I'm met with answers like:

"I'm not ready."

"It won't make a difference."

"I don't have what it takes."

"It's too late to follow my passion."

Fear. The answers are always based in fear. After asking these questions countless times to others—and seeing how they manifest in my own life—I've come to realize:

Every action we take in life is a direct result of the presence or absence of fear.

I speak with thousands of professionals each year: CEOs, high school grads, single parents, cancer patients, go-getters seeking advancement, tenured professionals seeking fulfillment, humans seeking permission to live with authenticity. Without fail, whether they make important shifts in behavior and thinking depends on whether or not they know how to manage their fear. Today's minds have built quantum computers and brought digital currency to the world, yet we still struggle to confront uncertainty and intimidation in our everyday life.

Too many people react to fear and shy away from harnessing the power within it. They make rash decisions based upon assumptions of what might go wrong. In many cases, become paralyzed with trepidation and make no decision at all.

This insistence of clinging to the status quo is not an adequate long-term solution. As imperfect humans existing in an imperfect society, we are faced with consistent and unrelenting change. It's what we do next that means the difference between a life well-lived and one spent running from the inevitable change of seasons.

You may be feeling the pull of a change (disruption) brewing. Maybe you have been contemplating a life or career change for some time now. Or maybe you just have an inkling of transformation on the horizon and you're not sure where to begin. Perhaps that is why you picked up this book. And if your instincts are correct, you're going to need some courage.

Visit therequisitecourage.com/bonusmaterials to download an exercise that will help you set your intention and find your focus for the next big change you are looking to make.

Change from any source brings disruption and opportunity. In this book, our energy will focus on change that stems from within. Examples and stories provided will emphasize the changes we decide to pursue—even with reservations—in order to seize the opportunity for growth and transformation. That being said, even those processing external change can benefit from the methodology and personal reflections to call out where fear is evident and how to mitigate the impact foreboding has on transition.

Chapter 2
Fortune Favors Failure

IIIIIIIIIIIIIIIIIIIIIII

In 1948, a question from his young daughter sparked Edwin H. Land to invent a camera that produced finished photographs in minutes. The invention was an immediate success and quickly took over the consumer and business markets. The instant camera was put into use for driver's licenses, crime reports, and holiday gifting. By the early 1970s, Polaroid held a monopoly in the instant photography market.

The 1990s brought with it emphasis on the digital film industry, but Polaroid leaders held strong to their belief that customers would always want a hard-copy print. CEO Israel MacAllister Booth crafted a 1985 letter to stockholders stating, "As electronic imaging becomes more prevalent, there remains a basic human need for a permanent visual record." Despite compelling market research to the contrary, Polaroid was unable to foresee that the family photo album would be replaced by the digital slide show. Film sales plummeted and Polaroid filed for bankruptcy in October 2001.[7]

Like Land and his successors, we've all held onto a belief for a bit too long.

Recall your last toxic relationship, when you started to see that you had outgrown the relationship but ignored the data your intuition was supplying, just like Polaroid execs ignored market research data. You were telling yourself, "I'm not a quitter," when in reality you were unwilling to see that a relationship that worked at first had stopped working.

Now expand your thinking of the term "relationship." When was the last time you experienced a toxic work culture? Are you in one now? Are you holding on to a string of hope that things will turn around, clinging to the idea that the current state of affairs will soon pass?

Beyond the status quo

In many ways for many reasons, we fool ourselves by attempting to create a world that is safe and predictable. We cling to what is familiar as the anxiety and helplessness that accompanies the fear of failure prompts us to stay safely inside our comfort zone. The terrifying unknown of change leads to full acceptance of the status quo.

Perhaps the most striking example of this comes from corporate America. Continuous tolerance of existing conditions in the workplace has led to what is now being termed "grind culture." Grind culture is the idea that status and success is achieved by always being "on." No matter where you are or what you are doing, you are to be perpetually available. You're reachable. Always hustling. The first thing you do when you open your eyes in the morning is check and respond to email. You are the first at the office and the last to leave. Sacrificing your personal time to complete a job task is a badge of honor.

RESEARCH SPOTLIGHT

Work addiction can be traced back to cultural norms that place high significance on work and career, even treating individuals according to their professional or material success. Researchers Peter Gahan and Lakmal Abeysekera found that national culture is an important determinant of how people see themselves at work, and many nations view hard work and occupational stress as a point of distinction.[8]

In a society where hard work is praised and putting in overtime is often expected, it can be difficult to recognize work addiction. People with a work addiction will often justify their behavior by explaining why it is a good thing and can help them achieve success. They may simply appear committed to their job or the success of their projects. However, ambition and addiction are quite different.

A person with a work addiction may engage in compulsive work to avoid other aspects of their life, like troubling emotional issues or personal crises. And similar to other addictions, the person may engage in the behavior unaware of the negative effects that the addiction is causing.

If you find yourself thinking of how you can free up more time to work, you spend more time working than you initially intend, or become stressed when you are not able to work, you may be trending toward addiction. You may consider making lifestyle changes, balancing life activities, and avoiding stressors and triggers to help.

Idolization of the workaholic is rampant in our culture and inside of our own minds. We don't want to let others down. Recent studies show that most people check their phones fifty-eight times per day with the average person spending upwards of eleven hours a day staring at a screen.[9] This connectivity fuels competition and favor for employees who make themselves available after hours. Furthermore, it limits—almost eliminates—the option of setting aside distraction to be fully present in other areas of life.

On the home front, the hustle culture has impacted entire generations of stay-at-home parents. Parental burnout is a diagnosable condition often described as exhaustion syndrome. Research has shown that the pressure women feel to achieve perfection in motherhood is related to maternal guilt, lower self-efficacy, and higher stress levels.[10] The pressure mounts so much so that failure becomes equated with any situation that is not achieved exactly as planned:

I threw a party **but** ran out of hors d'oeuvres.

I landed a big client at the office **but** missed my son's recital.

I took the family on a beach vacation **but** forgot to pack sunscreen.

It's almost as if it's too much, **but** it's never enough.

This chasing of the status quo creates an environment wherein many become paralyzed into procrastination and avoidance. Others opt to eventually jump off the never-ending merry-go-round. Still others fall off due to exhaustion. In this sense, failure often seems like the end of the line.

But what if instead of perpetuating a life in which we merely go along with business-as-usual and burn out in the process, we embraced life's unpredictability?

What if we faced life's inevitable failures to see what we might become?

What if we let go of the familiar to embrace the unknown?
Let's explore the benefits of this kind of abandonment.

The art of failing

You've heard, "Fortune favors the bold," but failure can also be a powerful catalyst for growth and success.

- Best-selling author Brian Tracy didn't graduate from high school but found his way to international success in sales and marketing, investing, real-estate development, and management consulting.
- Claude Monet received little but abuse from public and critics alike for his paintings before later being considered the founder of French Impressionism.
- It took James Dyson fifteen years and more than five thousand prototypes before having a vacuum he could present to British retailers, which was rejected.

We need to accept that we won't always make the right decisions, that we'll screw up royally sometimes— understanding that failure is not the opposite of success, it's part of success.
—Arianna Huffington

We learn so much when life goes off the rails and plans go array. Perspective is gained, important insights gathered, and our fortitude is put to the test. I often describe my first year as an entrepreneur akin to one's freshman year in college—investing an incredible amount of money and time, immersing myself in complete unpredictability, learning exponentially more with each missed marketing message or botched sales pitch than I could have from reading nine-hundred-and-ninety-nine business books.

To be honest, it took a lot of failing to learn some of the things I did back then.

I'm grateful (and humbled) to say the learning certainly didn't stop after year one. I continue to combat fears and failure every step along the way. Anyone who regularly rejects the status quo can say the same. Courage calls us to keep going. We must want growth more than we are afraid of pain.

If you find yourself standing in that space between—aspiring to growth but hesitant to face the pain—you're in the right place. The pages that follow will provide you with an instruction manual of sorts. Together, we will talk through practical, everyday concepts you can put into place to access the courage within you to face whatever comes your way. If you are a…

- successful doctor who longs to walk away from a lucrative career and begin again with passion…
- struggling spouse in a stifling marriage looking to finally take a stand…
- busy software developer caught up in the daily grind and struggling with self-worth weary to head back to the gym…
- brilliant author trying to conquer the inner demons and start finally writing that book…
- go-getter with an innovative business idea afraid to take the leap into entrepreneurship…
- recent grad preparing to move away from family for the first time…

…you will find actionable tools and exercises to step courageously into the future. Moving through the chapters ahead will give you confidence, momentum, and guidance as you weather the ups and downs that will accompany any one of these scenarios.

The choice is yours

Before we dive more deeply into each of the tenets of courage, I want to pause to remind you: you do have a choice. You do not have to activate the courage within. You do not have to seize the day. Giving into fear is always an option. It is 100% an option. Afraid you won't pass the bar exam? You can decide to quit law school and open a roadside stand selling strawberry jam. You recently lost your job? You can elect to head to the park each day in a suit and tie to feed geese rather than come clean to your family.

When I was facing limitations early in my career, I thought every day about breaking away to build a business. Yet the timing never seemed right. The finances weren't there. I questioned my own competency to achieve such a thing.

Staying put in a failing endeavor is certainly possible if that's what you choose. Not preferable, but possible. Staying stagnant, running from your fears, or walking away from an opportunity are all available to you. Hearing this may sting a bit. Acknowledging that you have a choice is part of the process of choosing courage. When the rubber meets the road, some turn back.

Even the famous quote, "Failure is not an option," is somewhat contrived. This quote is commonly attributed to Gene Kranz, Flight Director of NASA's Apollo 13 mission to the moon, but in fact, scriptwriters Al Reinert and Bill Broyles came up with this memorable line for the 1995 screenplay of their blockbuster movie Apollo 13. The seemingly stalwart words, "failure is not an option," were concocted from an interview with the crew. When asked, "Weren't there times when everybody, or at least a few people, just panicked?" flight controller Jerry Bostick responded, "When bad things happened, we just calmly laid out all the options....We never panicked, and we never gave up on finding a solution."[11]

You see, failure could have been an option. Giving up on the solution was an option. Giving into fear was an option. Mission failure was an option. The crew just chose not to take any of those options.

Life changes not because of what happens to you, but because of what you choose to do with what happens to you. Whatever the circumstances, however far the fall from grace, if you choose to build upon the loss and leverage the learning that accompanied a plan gone wrong, you did not fail. The story didn't end.

Fear factors

Our fears extend beyond fear of failure. Responses to anticipated or experienced disruption in life can include:

- Fear of rejection
- Fear of the unknown
- Fear of inadequacy
- Fear of isolation
- Fear of success

Let's break each of these down and identify where you may be facing resistance:

Fear of rejection

We feel timid and unsure, so we avoid confrontation. We ignore our own needs or pretend they don't matter. Apply to jobs beneath our paygrade. Avoid social situations or business dealings. Stay single and alone to escape stepping back into the dating scene. Engage in people pleasing behaviors, sacrificing ourselves for the happiness of those around us. We are convinced we will be denied what we want in life and that, somehow, depriving ourselves is less painful than facing the rejection of others

» At 8 years old, Alice Walker was shot in the right eye with a BB pellet while playing with two of her brothers. Whitish scar tissue formed in her damaged eye, and Walker largely withdrew from the world around her out of a fear of rejection. Fortunately for the world, she slowly put herself forward as a writer, essayist, and poet and eventually won the 1983 Pulitzer Prize for her extraordinary novel, *The Color Purple.*[12]

Fear of the unknown

We feel unsafe and at risk, so we shelter in place. We convince ourselves the sunk cost (the time/energy/money which has already been invested) dictates continued adherence to a plan that no longer serves us. We develop obsessive and/or compulsive tendencies and inflict strict rules on the people in our lives. We seek certainty and attempt to control even the most minute aspects of life. We place such a high value on order and predictability that we miss the forest for the trees.

» Brandon Stanton followed a career in finance after graduation, silencing his artistic side to build up a nest egg. After losing his job unexpectedly, he reconsidered his need to play it safe and began collecting photographs of everyday people in the city. *Humans of New York* quickly transformed from a simple Facebook page to a New York Times #1 Best Seller.[13]

Fear of inadequacy

We feel unworthy and ill-equipped, so we tell ourselves we are not enough. We are paralyzed by the fear of falling short. Pass on high-profile projects to avoid humiliation. Spend decades trying to prove we belong at the table without realizing we already have a seat. Seek frequent external validation but immediately invalidate it upon receipt. Enroll in continuous academic pursuits without stepping foot in the field. Underestimate our ability to perform. Downplay our accomplishments. Refuse to celebrate wins. We believe we are an impostor to our own lives, living in constant fear of being exposed as a fraud.

» Despite being invited to join the *Saturday Night Live* cast by Lorne Michaels himself, Aidy Bryant spent most of her first year fearing she would be fired. In an interview with Willie Geist, she disclosed that she "was crying all the time" convinced at any moment, "This is it, it's over." Now, after nine seasons on the show, the *SNL* veteran states that she focused on her personal strengths to get through the first intimidating year.[14]

Don't be afraid of your fears. They're not there
to scare you. They're there to let you know
that something is worth it.
—C. JoyBell C.

Fear of isolation

We feel unwanted and unloved, so we present ourselves in inauthentic ways in hopes of making people like us. We diminish the success of others in efforts to boost our own ego. Stay in unhealthy relationships to combat loneliness. Cry wolf to garner attention. Develop a harmful reliance on social media. Place ourselves in risky situations. We associate solitude with distress and take extreme measures to ensure we are always in the presence of others.

» NFL free agent Ryan Russell grew up in Texas where "football and religion" were all that mattered. After three years of keeping his true self hidden, he made the brave decision to come out as bisexual in August 2019. At the time of publishing, Russell is the only openly LGBTQ professional male athlete in the four major professional sports leagues.[15]

Fear of success

We feel secure and modest, so we accept the status quo. We limit ourselves so as to not upset others. Procrastinate. Have peers take credit for our work. Self-sabotage. Silence the good disruption. Fail to speak up when treated unfairly. Set the bar low to keep ourselves from being challenged. Set up roadblocks. Fear being knocked off the pedestal we didn't want to be on in the first place. We set a standard too high to be reached, pointing to the inevitable shortfall as reason enough not to proceed.

» Reshma Saujani worked at a law firm and then in finance, and even ran for Congress. She acknowledges chasing a paycheck in jobs she hated for decades before going after her true passion. In 2021, she founded Girls Who Code, an international non-profit on track to close the gender gap in new-entry level tech jobs by 2030.[16]

Now, I can't say for sure how these overcomers were feeling as they faced fear, but their stories of trial and ultimate triumph certainly showcase the external indicators we would expect to see.

If you see yourself in the stories of Reshma, Aidy, Brandon, and Ryan, don't worry. It means you are human like the rest of us. We'll address each of these fears and other limiting beliefs in the chapters ahead. You will have the opportunity to identify which roadblocks you encounter the most and formulate an action plan to minimize their effect on your pursuits. Together, we will explore the means to determine when change is needed and discuss a simple structure for building resilience in the face of perpetual disruption.

Visit therequisitecourage.com/bonusmaterials to take the Fear Factor quiz and identify which fears are stopping you in your tracks and what you can do to eliminate those roadblocks.

Chapter 3

Accessing Courage

||||||||||||||||||||||

I don't have the cure for fear. I am neither a scientist nor a physician with decades of research behind a groundbreaking discovery that can package boldness in a neat little pill to be swallowed and dispersed through your veins. Some days, when my inner saboteur is particularly loud, I don't think I have any answers.

I am an ordinary person who has faced some extraordinary tests of courage: jumping out of a plane, traversing a seventeen-hundred-year-old cave dwelling, and dog sledding on a glacier. I've also faced less glamorous but more life-defining fears: the suicide of someone close to me, a painful divorce, and starting and restarting a business.

AUTHOR SPOTLIGHT

While terrified of heights, I've actually jumped out of three different planes on three different occasions.

My first dive was to show my mom that I was paying attention. Noticing what she had taught me and behaviors she was continuing to model. You see, my mother raised me to believe that every story is worth living. She believes one should seize adventure and live life to the fullest. As such, it was only right that I presented her with a bucket-list experience on the day of her college graduation (a whole other story about my mom being a maverick is how she obtained her bachelor's degree two days after she turned fifty).

The second jump took place on a visit to Key West. The view from miles above the ocean was breathtaking—clear blue waters and white sandy beaches. My adrenaline was pumping so hard when I landed back on solid ground that I almost couldn't process my soulmate down on one knee with a ring in his hand.

My third leap was in celebration of my first major business milestone. When I first quit my job, a good friend and advisor asked me what I feared most. I thought for a minute, then shared that I was afraid I would give up on the business before replacing my six-figure income. I posed the same question back, "What are you most afraid of?" He revealed a desire to, but desperate fear of, jumping out of a plane. I challenged him to skydive with me when I hit one hundred thousand dollars in revenue. We shook on it. Two years later, we jumped at twenty thousand feet.

I have found through life trials and tribulations that choosing courage, even when I am afraid, more often than not has led me closer to the life I want. In select cases, choosing courage brought forth outcomes I desperately needed and wasn't even aware were possible. In more than one instance, I actively chased after the fear, trusting that just beyond it lay some of the most amazing experiences I would have in my life.

Through it all, I discovered a straightforward approach to building resiliency in the face of doubt. Activating courage begins with understanding your heart through increased self-awareness and commitment to purpose. From here, you learn to embrace change with a growth mindset and gain the confidence to follow your heart. Finally, you step into action with intention, accountability, and resilience. By employing these tenets in my own life, I learned to harness the power of fear to combat impostor syndrome, confront resistance head on, and live courageously.

Now I invite you to do the same. There is a path through the valley of change and fear. I can't promise it will be easy, but I commit that if you apply this solution to your own journey, you will find a way to live with authenticity and audacity.

Accessing the requisite courage to move through the fear and into change requires three steps: Clarity, Conviction, and Constancy.

The three Cs of courage

Clarity

The source of courage comes from within. This is well known. But the lesser-known detail is that it literally comes from who you are. Inner strength comes from having clarity around who you are and what you want. Encourage a new path to your why to crystalize and focus all your energy on that which feeds your mission. You have to gain clarity in order to gain momentum towards your next objective—even when that goal is to simply identify what the next goal post should be.

Conviction

Living in alignment with your mission requires letting go of that which does not serve you and embracing what does. Trust that a purpose built on values allows you to pivot to new directions as needed. Rest and reset in knowing that while the plan may have gone up in smoke, your deeper purpose need not. Employing a growth mindset and allowing the smoldering ashes to glow and light the way to new possibilities.

And that final step:

Constancy

Employ endurance. Establish daily practices that breed resolve and build resilience. The quality of endurance is that of getting up, again and again, no matter how many times you fall. When we commit to that constancy, we give ourselves permission to take any step—even small and seemingly insignificant strides—in the right direction. Reevaluating the plan at frequent intervals. Burning the plan when needed. Being open to new plans. Embracing the disruptive moments.

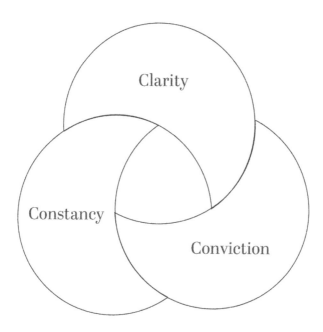

The call for courage keeps coming. Reassess. Reconnect. Rebuild. Lather. Rinse. Repeat. Each time with more capacity for courage and greater outcomes. Relish in the knowledge and perspective gained from blunders and bombs. In many ways, the ashes from my past helped to build the foundation of my home, my business, and the way I look at the world. The way the world looks at me.

Enduring. Doing. Living with courage. These concepts are introduced and put to the test with stories of risk and resilience and opportunities for self-application in the chapters to come.

Fearless execution

In the days, weeks, and months ahead, you will see a rate of change like never before. Futurist Ray Kurzweil discerns that, "Mankind is on the cusp of a radically accelerating era of change unlike anything we have ever seen and almost more extreme than we can imagine."[17] What an incredible time to be alive. And you are uniquely positioned to decide if you will embrace that change or fight against it.

The twisted nature of our personal and professional journeys often takes us to terrifying yet beautiful places. Even when you are on a path you trust from deep within is the "right" course, it can be daunting. Stepping into fear can illuminate a new and exciting reality. When you face the unknown with courage, you trade predictability for possibility; career stability for career agility; chaos for opportunity.

Stand in the dark or turn on the light. The choice is yours, but as a leader, the impact of your decision is exponential. When you turn on a light, others begin to see. Consider the massive mindset shift you can create at home and at work in your own approach. Simply by responding to disruption with a nod of good fortune. By embracing the opportunities it presents.

The secret to authentic living and leading is not in flawless strategy; it is in fearless execution.

Turn on the light for yourself, find your courage, and others will benefit from your shine. THIS is a time to amplify that ripple effect while our world is paying attention and people are craving connection. Give it to them.

Fear drives our lives. Fortunately, with some practice, you can learn to access the courage that drives fear away.

Courage in Action

Setting Your Intention

As we step together into the tenants of courage, I want to call you into action. Rather than simply considering the principles shared from an overview, let's dive into specifics. Any worthwhile journey starts with identifying a destination. The exercise below will help you to outline a specific change you are facing or want to make, and subsequent exercises throughout the book will guide you through the application of each step to that change. By the end of our time together, you will be on your way to transformation.

Think about the changes you are facing right now or know that you want to make within the next year and write those down.

_____

_____

_____

_____

Given time, I'm sure you can think about plenty of things you'd like to improve or overhaul altogether, but from the changes you have identified above, circle the one change you want to make in your life right now.

Then, from the categories listed below, circle the category that best fits the change you have selected.

- Business & Career
- Money & Finances
- Health & Fitness
- Mind & Emotions
- Family
- Romance & Intimate Relationships
- Personal Growth

- Friends & Fun
- Other _____

With the category you have identified above in mind, get down to the specifics of the situation—what is it that needs to change? What aspect of this area would you like to see change? Capture all your thoughts—especially those that immediately come to mind, but you find yourself pushing back from—no idea is too big or too small.

Ex. My biggest problem is in the Health and Fitness category. I would like to lose some weight, feel better, fit into my clothes, have more energy, work out more, etc.

_____

_____

The Fear Factor

The below quiz will help you identify which of the five fear factors has the greatest impact on the way you respond to change. While you may struggle with all types of fear at one point or another, it's helpful to identify some strongholds now as you begin your journey into courage. These fear factors can become limiting beliefs, which are beliefs that we tell ourselves that are often negative and get in the way of change and growth.

Each should have a rating Always (5) – Often (4) – Sometimes (3) – Rarely (2) – Never (1)

1. ____ I engage in people-pleasing behaviors, prioritizing the happiness of others above myself.
2. ____ I have a vested interest in maintaining the status quo.

3. _____ I do what it takes to make others like me.

4. _____ I steer clear of confrontation to avoid upsetting others.

5. _____ I try to control the situations I am in and the people that surround me.

6. _____ I tell lies and/or exaggerate the truth to gain attention.

7. _____ I refute positive feedback given by others.

8. _____ I set unreasonable goals and standards for myself.

9. _____ I tell myself no so as not to have to hear it from someone else.

10. _____ I crave order and structure.

11. _____ Being alone makes me nervous.

12. _____ I refuse to celebrate my own success.

13. _____ I hold myself back to avoid failure and looking bad in front of others in order to make others feel more comfortable.

14. _____ I often doubt my skills and abilities to perform despite a proven track record.

15. _____ I procrastinate to avoid imperfection.

16. _____ I am uncomfortable with change

17. _____ I thrive with predictability

18. _____ No matter how much I achieve, I never feel like it is enough.

19. _____ I overstate past successes on my resume to be more marketable

20. _____ I fear being excluded from recognition.

Assess your *fear of rejection* by tallying your responses for questions 1, 3, 4, 9 _____

Assess your *fear of isolation* by tallying your responses for questions 6, 11, 19, 20 _____

Assess your *fear of success* by tallying your responses for questions 2, 7, 8, 12 _____

Assess your *fear of inadequacy* by tallying your responses for questions 13, 14, 15, 18 _____

Assess your *fear of unknown* by tallying your responses for questions 5, 10, 16, 17 _____

Evaluating your fears above, which impact you the most? You might have two that stand out, you might have three, or you might be impacted by all five fears.

_____

_____

What are you missing out on because of these fears or limiting beliefs? How are these fears getting in the way of change?

Ex. I don't always give my best effort or participate in activities I would benefit from.

_____

_____

Spend a moment contemplating what your life will look like when you conquer these fears and achieve your desired change.

Ex. I would feel free. I would go places I am currently too shy/afraid to visit. I would be a better role model for my kids.

_____

_____

Identifying the **area of change** you desire and the **fear(s)** holding you back is a crucial step before moving forward in this book. Record them below.

Change You Desire _____
Ex. Exercise consistently

Fear Holding You Back _____
Ex. Fear of Unknown, inadequacy

Seriously, don't read another page if you haven't taken the time to complete the above exercises.

Yes, it's that important.

Keep your desired change and identified fears top of mind as we move through subsequent sections. Specific exercises will be offered to help apply each tenet to your situation and put courage in action.

By the end of the book, you will have a customized guide for stepping through your fears and into courageous change.

You are in the driver's seat of this journey. It's never or now.

Ready, Set, Courage!

Part 2:

Clarity

clar·i·ty/ˈklerˈdē/

noun: the quality of being coherent and intelligible.

Chapter 4
Light and Dark

||||||||||||||||||||||||||

I can still hear his words: "I will kill myself if I can't have you."

"Go ahead. I don't care," I replied, exhausted by the late-night call and tired of his attempts to control me and my decisions with emotional manipulation.

In poker, the objective of a bluff is to induce a fold by your opponent who holds a better hand. The size and frequency of a bluff determine its profitability to the bluffer. By extension, the phrase "calling somebody's bluff" is often used outside the context of poker to describe situations where one person demands that another proves a claim or proves that they are not being deceptive.

Moments after I hung up the phone, my high school sweetheart died by suicide. Shot himself straight into the roof of his mouth, plunging a bullet into his skull, blowing his brains out the back of his head. His life was gone and so was my innocence.

The days that followed are blurry, although not because they happened almost three decades ago. Rather, they are forever painted with a broad brush, allowing both light and dark to creep in behind the memories. What I distinctly recall was feeling overrun with panic due to the utter lack of control suddenly thrust upon my life. Well-meaning people started to ask me what I was going to do as if I had been prepped for such a horrific ordeal. Adversaries began asking me what I had done, as though the romantic whims of a seventeen-year-old could justify a tragic suicide.

As a young adult, just when I was starting to figure out who I was and what I stood for, this egregious act came and wiped that all away. I was being called to a level of courage I wasn't even aware existed, let alone one I could manifest within myself. I went from stressing over test scores to pondering the ripple effect: How perfect would I need to be in future relationships and endeavors to avoid causing such destruction again? I felt scared and confused. I thought I was to blame for his actions. I knew I was the last person to speak to him. I didn't know he was capable of such a thing.

Grasping for meaning

The questions. The accusations. The grief. The reality that he was gone. It all quickly became completely unbearable. Whatever was left of my childhood had been stripped away. The leisurely process of growth and development that accompanied adolescence was abruptly replaced with an unrelenting requirement for emotional, social, and intellectual maturity. This unwelcome change was crushing. The need for conscious courage was pressing, but the confusion of where to begin was overwhelming. It felt as though all eyes were on me, anxiously awaiting my next move.

Among the chaos, I found myself clutching for something real. I needed something to ground me. I scrambled to locate something reliable from which I could build a steady base. In a world turned seemingly upside down, I turned to the only thing I could command—myself.

I began to look inward for stability. The death and subsequent reaction of everyone around me had left me skeptical and I knew I could depend on myself. Though it wasn't long before I realized I needed more information to maintain that reliability. In a place in time where everyone else seemed to have an opinion about who I was and what I should do, I began asking myself those same questions: *Who am I?*

A solid decision-maker.

Strong.

Stubborn.

Not so much an eternal optimist but a lemonade maker.

Resourceful. Rational. Resilient.

Restoring my sense of self not only led me to find my next steps but also strengthened my resolve to live with purpose. Deep down, I had a desire to cultivate something beautiful from such an ugly act. I wanted to balance the negative with a positive outcome. When I turned off all the outside noise, I realized I would be ok. I trusted myself to come out of this alive and perhaps even better for having done so.

Why do I share this vulnerable story about my young adult self?

At the time, I had no idea this event would bring meaning to my life. It illuminated my passion for guiding others through change. My tolerance for tackling the unknown. My tendency and commitment to return things/people/circumstances to a stable state. My deep belief in stepping up when the world brings you down.

It also taught me a critical aspect of courage that is often over-looked. The source of courage comes from within. This is well known. But the lesser-known detail is that it literally comes from who you are. Every slice of courage—whether great or small—is grounded in clarity around who you are and what you want.

Chapter 5
Recognize Patterns

IIIIIIIIIIIIIIIIIIIIII

We established in previous chapters that change, whether invited or unexpected, is inevitable. Now let us explore more about the process that happens after the change is in motion. This will help us to make sense of the steps we take when change is introduced and illuminate our instinctual behavior in the timeframe thereafter.

The Change Curve is a graphic representation of the five stages of reacting to change. Elisabeth Kübler-Ross originally developed the model by studying the patterns in the various levels of emotions of a person experiencing near death. It has since been widely adapted for use in business given its validity in the majority of cases and situations related to change.

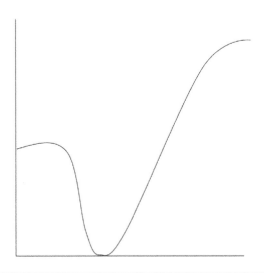

RESEARCH SPOTLIGHT[18]

Since the 1980s, companies have relied upon the change curve to predict how performance is likely to be affected by the announcement and subsequent implementation of a significant change in the workplace.

The first reaction to change is typically shock and denial due to lack of information and fear of the unknown. While frequently short-lived, this initial shock can result in a temporary slowdown and loss of productivity. In this stage, communication is key. Leaders can support team members by reiterating what the actual change is, the effects it may have, and providing reassurance to those particularly affected.

The second stage encompasses anger and often involves staff identifying a scapegoat to blame. This blame allows for continued denial but with a new focus. Team members may turn to suspicious and/or skeptical behavior. When the anger begins to wear off and a realization that the change is, in fact, going to occur, anxiety follows. It is common during this stage for morale to be low and apathy to peak. Feeling separated from a common goal, individuals may fixate on small issues or problems. Discussing the shared emotions of isolation and frustration can help to develop a more stable platform from which to move to the final stage.

The final response to change brings a more optimistic and enthusiastic mood. Team members begin to accept that change is inevitable and being to work with the changes rather than against them. Primary feelings center around hope and trust as individuals become excited by new opportunities and are relieved to have survived the change. As the organization moves through this third stage, energy and productivity remain low but slowly show signs of improvement. Everyone will have lots of questions and be curious about the possibilities that lie ahead. Team members will benefit from being given specific tasks and regular progress reports.

The five stages in the original model include denial, anger, bargaining, depression, and acceptance. While numbered, individuals facing change rarely move along the stages in a linear direction nor do they follow a step-by-step approach. A person can and will likely move back and forth between stages in a random order, staying within each emotional state for a variable amount of time. Let's explore each stage in more detail:

1. Denial

The initial stage of shock or denial is intense but mostly short-lived. During this phase, one puts on a temporary defense mechanism while taking the time to process certain disturbing news or reality. Denial can bring about a dip in productivity and in one's ability to think and act.

2. Anger

When the realization finally sets in and the gravity of the situation becomes known, one can become angry and may look for someone to blame. Anger may be expressed in various ways, sometimes directed inward and in other instances directed towards others around them. This stage is marked by irritability and frustration.

3. Bargaining

As the anger passes, one begins to reach for ways to postpone the inevitable. This may involve desperate negotiations and or attempts at compromise. Bargaining may help to come to a sustainable solution and might bring some relief, yet the search for a different outcome—and failure to recognize one might not exist—may remain ongoing.

4. Depression

Depression is a stage in which the person tends to feel sadness, fear, regret, and/or guilt. Displaying signs of indifference and reclusiveness, one may have completely given up and become engulfed in darkness. This may seem like a dead end.

5. Acceptance

With the passing of time, the tides change, and people come to accept that no amount of fighting the change will make it go away. They resign themselves to the situation and begin to move ahead with it.

An example that hits close to home for many is job loss resulting from the global pandemic. The following scenario clearly demonstrates the transition process from one stage to another:

Tanya had been working as a choreographer for the Broadway Theatre since completing her internship straight out of college. She loved her work, finding the right balance between her love for dance and her eye for entertainment. Three weeks after the CDC announced the shutdown of venues in New York City, Tanya was furloughed along with eighty-five percent of her coworkers.

1. Denial: Tanya's first reaction was that of absolute shock. She could not believe everything she had worked so hard for had come to an abrupt halt, especially now when she needed the income more than ever.

2. Anger: Once she realized there was no easy fix to the problem, Tanya became infuriated. She started spending all her time on social media, scrolling through news feeds and blaming the government, CDC, corporate America—anyone she could think of who could have contributed to the situation.

3. Bargaining: Tanya called her boss and requested he reconsider. Begged him to give her a chance to work in advanced ticket sales until the pandemic passed. When rejected, she started calling all her friends, asking if their crew had any openings.

4. Depression: As reality set in, Tanya's mind filled with negative thoughts. She began to feel depressed, sad, and hopeless. She feared she may never work again, and she would have to give up her apartment and move back home to her parents in Wisconsin.

5. Acceptance: After processing her grief, Tanya began to access information on the unemployment benefits being offered through the government, as well as rent relief programs being offered in her community. She started working with a coach to identify possible bridge jobs that would provide income until the theaters were safe to open again.

When change is thrust upon you, like Tanya, it is easy to feel as though you are drowning. Uncertainty, ambiguity, indecisiveness, anxiety, and stress start to overwhelm the system. Even as you attempt to negotiate your way to a different circumstance, you are acutely aware of the void (ex. lack of time, love, direction, certainty, etc.) the change has created. Searching for meaning in the disruption, you often come up empty-handed.

To work through her grief and despair, Tanya had to dig deep. She needed to acknowledge the pain and anger to move through it. Her acceptance came with time, but also an understanding of her inherent capabilities and the opportunities she could create. While the layoffs happened to her, they did not define her.

In the face of change, we must follow Tanya's lead. We must turn within and grasp for self-knowledge to begin to accept the change so that we can summon the courage to face it.

Know thyself

The craving for self-analysis dates back to ancient Greece. Apollo, son of Zeus, was recognized as the god of truth and prophecy (among other things). According to legend, a stone at the entrance to Apollo's temple at Delphi contained a carving that read:

KNOW THYSELF

The age-old consensus of the importance of self-knowledge likely stems from the view that authenticity is an honest and therefore morally superior way of being.[19] This explains that undeniable pit in our stomachs when we fail to follow our intuition, or the sense of discontent when we place a higher priority on pleasing others than following our own path. Being true to thine own self is experienced as a form of virtue.

Early philosophers, such as Plato, Hippocrates, and Galen, explored individual differences in personal traits and behaviors. Scholars and theorists have since continued this self-analysis for centuries. Seventeenth-century philosopher John Locke postulated that we begin life with a *tabula rasa* (blank slate) upon which a series of sensory perceptions can be impressed, leading to rational application.

David Hume, also an empiricist, believed our personal identities are merely a bundle of experiences, perceptions, and memories. According to Friedrich Nietzsche in the late 1800s, "know thyself" means something more like recognizing and embracing individuality. Existentialist Jean-Paul Sartre marked twentieth-century philosophy by imploring humans to define their own lives and use free will to create a sense of meaning.

When your values are clear to you, making decisions becomes easier. Our values drive our purpose. Our purpose drives action. Action drives results. Your path to stepping through fear and into courageous change needs to be grounded in your true self—in what you value and what you stand for. Any other route will trigger self-sabotage, and the self-induced roadblocks of procrastination and avoidance will be insurmountable.

Chapter 6
Embark on Self Discovery

|||||||||||||||||||||||

G aining an understanding of your character traits, core values, motivations, and desires requires intention. While you may have awareness of some personality traits and firmly held beliefs, many of your core characteristics and personal views have been functioning under the surface.

Earlier, we outlined the pitfalls of basing your identity in what you do or who you care for. The deep work of self-discovery is the cornerstone to living a life that is driven by confidence and ownership over your individual purpose. Increased awareness of your character, feelings, motives, and desires illuminates the unique value that you bring to the world. This awareness also highlights the unique value that the world so desperately needs *from* you.

Bringing these attributes to light can be an exciting and fulfilling endeavor.

Objective assessments

Thanks to the efforts of countless psychologists, business leaders, and other brilliant minds, individuals today have a plethora of easily accessible tools to support self-discovery. In fact, personality testing is roughly a five-hundred-million-dollar industry wherein results are often leveraged to help professionals predict potential roadblocks, improve collaboration, and identify satisfying career paths. Assessments are a great place to start if you are looking for a focus of study, career direction, greater understanding of your strengths and weaknesses, and improved relationships with others. Most importantly, they make self-discovery accessible for those who may not know where to start.

You may be a certified administrator of personality tests or have merely dabbled in a few online quizzes to date. Either way, I have described the most popular and longest-standing self-assessments below.

Myers-Briggs

The Myers-Briggs Type Indicator is a self-report questionnaire that takes an introspective look at differing psychological preferences in how people perceive the world and make decisions. First published in 1962, the test attempts to assign four categories: introversion (I) or extraversion (E), sensing (S) or intuition (N), thinking (T) or feeling (F), judging (J) or perceiving (P).[20]

DISC

The DISC Model of Behavior was first proposed in 1928 by William Moulton Marston, a physiological psychologist, in his book *Emotions of Normal People*. DISC is a behavior self-assessment tool centered on four personality traits: Dominance, Influence, Steadiness, and Compliance. These traits reveal patterns of behavior in various situations such as response to challenges, ability to influence others, preferred pace, and acceptance of rules and procedures.[21]

Keirsey Temperament Sorter
The Keirsey questionnaire was developed in 1978 by educational psychologist David Keirsey. The KTS provides insight into temperament and personality related to both personal and professional matters. The resulting types address how temperament and personality impact leadership, the workplace, teamwork, selling and buying, marketing, learning, careers, and romance.[22]

Enneagram of Personality
The Enneagram personality test came into its current form through a series of psychologists and spiritual teachers throughout the second half of the twentieth century. The results are displayed using the distinct enneagram figure and show different categories of personalities numbered one through nine. Each number represents a different personality type with unique characteristics, strengths, weaknesses, motivations, and fears.[23]

Subjective assessments
The above are examples of powerful tools that provide valuable insight into your mindset, behavior, relationship preferences, personality traits, etc. If objective assessments aren't your thing, you can still learn what feeds you by analyzing your experiences. Some simple reflection or a synergistic conversation with a curious companion can uncover trends in your mannerisms and motivations. You need only a safe space to hear your own voice.

If you are a traveler, consider how you choose where to go and what you do when you arrive. Are you more of a planner or a spontaneous tourist? Are you the type who seeks out adventure, renting a bike to traverse central Europe, or sitting at a quiet cafe to digest the world?

If you are a writer, think about your content of choice. Do you find your best ideas in the minutia of day-to-day life or when inspired by grandiose notions? Are your works grounded in realism and research, or do they wistfully explore a mythical land?

If you are a teacher, ponder your favorite format. Are you inspired by a classroom of eager young faces or the challenge of teaching an old dog new tricks? Do you seize impromptu opportunities to share wisdom and guide others, or are you at your best in a formal setting with well-defined space and time?

If you are a leader, reflect on your approach to directing others. Do you enjoy getting down into the trenches with servant leadership or rely on power and experience to dictate who does the work? Are you more likely to be found analyzing data or translating strategy? Do you maintain an open-door policy or prefer direct reports to self-manage?

If you are a caregiver, review your greatest moments of connection. Do you use humor when the going gets tough, or do you provide calm in moments of stress? Do you gather a support team to help, or do you take the solo advocate approach for your loved ones?

Your responses to the questions above (and similar reflections) can provide you immense insight into your character, capabilities, and motivations. A wealth of self-knowledge is found by simply bringing intention and awareness to one's natural preferences. This treasure trove of insight connects us to who we are and sheds light on why we do what we do. Each organic decision is rooted in a unique code of values that serves as a compass for your journey.

The name of my company, Professional Courage, pays homage to a moment of insight into my own unique code. Early in my career, I worked as a project manager for a health maintenance organization. I was often sent into departments and areas where I didn't know anyone, where people (most often doctors) had a lot more power and distinction than I did. Yet, I would go almost blind to my rank and do what was needed to rally the troops and influence decisions being made for a better bottom-line outcome. My supervisor told me I had *professional courage*—the ability to walk into a room with unexpected confidence rooted in fierce determination to achieve the outlined goal. Somehow stepping into new territory with that confidence gave permission to others to do the same. That attribute is now the foundation of my life's work.

Beyond stepping up to challenges and pushing past limitations, self-awareness allows for the management of oneself and proper pursuit of strengths in the marketplace. When people are willing to pursue their natural tendencies instead of struggling against them, they often uncover a path to great success that they wouldn't have been able to find any other way.

The great singer/songwriter Andrea Bocelli started his career as a lawyer. He worked part-time at a piano bar as an outlet for his love of music. He is now the most popular classical singer in history.

Ben Silbermann says his childhood penchant for collecting bugs inspired Pinterest, an online catalog of ideas with an estimated worth of over eleven billion dollars.

Jack Dorsey co-founded Twitter after growing up with a speech impediment. A very shy child, he never felt comfortable having normal face-to-face conversations with people. Now, the world talks to one another in 280-character spurts over five hundred million times a day.

The link between who you are and what you do cannot be overstated. When our energy and effort is concentrated on our natural gifts, we are better equipped—and more motivated—to bring substantial impact to the organizations and communities in which we serve. An organic bravery comes from our authentic self, almost as though the universe is working in our favor. Discover who you truly are and fully give every aspect of your uniqueness to the world. Establishing a clear understanding of who you are and what you value (and we'll discuss that more in the next section) will lead you undoubtedly down a path of courageous action in the direction of your desired change.

Core values

As you contemplate the various roles you have served and continue to serve in, give some thought to the core values that drive your decisions. Values are defined as the principles or standards that are most important to us - whether known outright or hidden inside our behaviors and priorities. When we narrow down the wide variety of personal values to find the core ones that define us, we gain even greater clarity around past and future choices.

Are you quick to forgive a coworker for failing to pull their weight to restore harmony?

Do you prioritize requests based upon the hierarchical position of the requestor, deferring to power?

Would you opt for a tenured position even if it meant a lower salary over time to guarantee job security?

Do you approach family matters by attempting to understand and share the feelings of another?

Use the list below to review and focus on those values that guide your daily actions. Identify which traits come to mind most often when you are in a place of decision making or discernment. Place a checkmark next to all those that resonate.

Take this introspection a step further and rank order your top ten. Circle the top five values that are most meaningful to you in life and work. We will refer back to these values in future exercises around your deeper motivations.

Accountability	Creativity	Hard work
Achievement	Curiosity	Harmony
Adaptability	Decisiveness	Health
Adventure	Democracy	Honesty
Assertiveness	Dependability	Honor
Authenticity	Determination	Humility
Authority	Dignity	Humor
Autonomy	Discipline	Independence
Balance	Diversity	Individuality
Beauty	Empathy	Influence
Belonging	Endurance	Integrity
Boldness	Enjoyment	Intelligence
Calmness	Equality	Joy
Challenge	Exploration	Justice
Citizenship	Fairness	Kindness
Commitment	Faith	Knowledge
Community	Fame	Leadership
Compassion	Family	Learning
Competency	Financial Security	Love
Competitiveness	Freedom	Loyalty
Connection	Friendships	Making a Difference
Contentment	Fun	Meaningful Work
Contribution	Generosity	Openness
Conviction	Goodness	Optimism
Cooperation	Growth	Peace
Courage	Happiness	Pleasure

Poise	Self-Respect	Structure
Popularity	Selflessness	Success
Power	Service	Teamwork
Recognition	Simplicity	Trustworthiness
Religion	Skillfulness	Truth
Reputation	Spirituality	Wealth
Respect	Stability	Wisdom
Responsibility	Status	Wonder
Security	Strength	

Visit therequisitecourage.com/bonusmaterials to download an exercise that shines a light on the values most closely aligned with your desired change.

Heightened awareness

So far, we have explored several ways you can begin to find clarity through introspective work done on your own. Taking an honest look at your personality traits and core values also demands some outside input.

For all its negative connotations, well-thought-out feedback from a trusted source is a tremendous tool for the process of self-discovery. Feedback incentivizes learning and enhances our ability to self-regulate. Feedback from others can offer a window into our soul. We tend to hold on to our beliefs and assumptions in the absence of evidence to the contrary. Obtaining an outside viewpoint can help us see our intention—our self view—mirrored back to us.

RESEARCH SPOTLIGHT

John Baird and Edward Sullivan, executives at the Velocity Group, have spent years searching for the secret to leadership. With a client list of top leaders at Fortune 500 companies including Apple, Nike, and Twitter, they have narrowed in on what it takes to excel in leadership and life.

"The most effective, transformative leaders we've worked with are exquisitely curious," Sullivan stated in a recent interview with CNBC. "They're always asking questions when something doesn't work out: they want to know why, and what could we be doing differently to solve the problem."[24]

Without curiosity, leaders wouldn't have the drive to gather new information and stay up to date with the current industry trends. Moreover, when curious leaders face unique challenges, they ask relevant questions. They listen to other team members, thus setting the right mood for constructive discussions. The strongest problem solvers are those who know enough and are open to thinking outside the box.

Interpretation of our actions through another's eyes isn't simply about past performance, it can also inform future capability. Constructive criticism is essential for growth. Learning from feedback reduces your blind areas—facets of your life wherein you may not be displaying your standards as intended. Once these blind spots are exposed, you can diagnose the root of the discrepancy and alter behaviors accordingly. Acting in alignment with your core values is a necessary building block to stepping through the fear and into courageous change.

Your assumptions are your windows on the world...
Scrub them off every once in a while, or the light
won't come through.

—Isaac Asimov

Review the top five values you circled in the Core Values section. Ask yourself: Do you live these values to your family? Friends? Coworkers? Clients? Are these the same words they would use to describe your fundamental drivers?

If you're not sure what they would say:

Ask them. Incorporate external feedback to heighten your self-awareness wherever and whenever possible. Pursue a formal 360-degree survey or simply send an email to your key contacts asking for some quick thoughts on what you do well and where you can improve.

Who will you ask?

What specific questions will you pose?

What format will you use to send the request (phone call, email, survey tool)?

Remember to also set aside some time to review and digest the feedback received.

If you think their answers would be in contrast to your authentic self:

Set aside time for self-reflection and contemplate the answers to the questions below.

Where do you find it challenging to live in alignment?

What underlying fears are stopping you from bringing your true self to the table? (Refer back to the quiz you completed at the end of Part One to help identify your strongest fears.)

How might you work through these barriers?

Who can you lean upon as an accountability partner to begin to step more confidently into your authenticity?

If/when you do feel as though your personal values and strengths are being shown to the world, congrats. Now let's keep it that way. Set a reminder to reassess every six months and ensure things continue to be in alignment.

Chapter 7
Fear of Rejection

||||||||||||||||||||||||||

It's not uncommon to face roadblocks as you move into clarity. By articulating what you stand for, you simultaneously invite a response from others while the fear of rejection increases.

For many, this fear triggers people-pleasing behaviors. You may find yourself ignoring your own needs or sacrificing yourself for the happiness of those around you. It's a dangerous game to play—living life for others' expectations and happiness instead of your own.

People pleasers often deal with low self-esteem and draw their self-worth from the approval of others. You might also have a strong desire to be needed, believing that you have a better chance of receiving affection from people who need you. You worry that telling someone "No" will make them think you don't care about them, and so you agree to do what they want even when you don't have the time or inclination. Trying to earn the regard of others usually means you neglect your own needs and feelings.

The fear of rejection often rears its ugly head in a specific people-pleasing behavior known as perfectionism. Affected individuals believe that operating without error will allow one to avoid the pain of being left behind.

But perfection is a fallacy.

In his famous novel *East of Eden*, John Steinbeck wrote, "And now that you don't have to be perfect, you can be good."[25] His characters were speaking to the plight of perfection, the unattainable myth that we fool—sometimes outright lie to—ourselves in believing we have attained. Struggling to achieve flawless execution forces us to live in a heightened state of urgency and tension. Chasing perfection can be paralyzing, affecting our mental health and quality of life.

How many times have you avoided a situation altogether out of fear of being subpar?

My coaching clients share countless stories of not speaking up at a meeting, not going for a promotion, not volunteering for a desired project out of fear they aren't perfectly prepared. The act of stepping into the project to get their feet wet leaves them too exposed.

As kids we suffered endless baseball and baritone practices, hearing again and again that this consistent application was the only way to learn and improve a new skill. However, as adults, we seem to have forgotten these lessons and feel we should be hitting balls out of the park on day one. No time for learning, only success. Chasing perfection does not allow for the very growth and development that will take us to that next level.

Authentic living

Dedicating our behavioral impulses to the favor of others imposes a belief that our true selves are not or would not be valued. The contrary is true. Researchers found that people who scored higher on a measure of authentic living reported greater happiness, more positive emotions, and higher self-esteem than people who reported being less authentic. More authentic people also reported having better relationships with others and more personal growth.[26]

Genuine people offer a genuine response to what is happening around them; they do not hide their feelings or pretend they are feeling something they are not. The focus of living with authenticity is always about you and your own journey, without seeking the validation of others. When you are embracing authenticity, you refrain from lying or misleading others and become comfortable within your own, unique skin.

One of the most powerful tactics for practicing truth is to live in the present. Avoid allowing the past to dictate your future. Rather than worry about repeating past mistakes, free yourself to create new experiences and new relationships. Those living authentically attract people who are doing the same. These connections help build confidence and promote both parties to bring their best selves to the table.

CLIENT SPOTLIGHT

Coaching directors within the same organization provides a unique lens through which to view entire business units and their management approach. When various professionals all reference the same leader with similar feedback, it can be hard to ignore.

I partner with a global automation firm to provide executive coaching to senior leaders. Sessions are focused on enhancing personal brand positioning and preparing for advancement within the organization. I often inquire as to outstanding role models within the organization and dissect the attributes they embody. For years, the same executive has been noted by each director for building a strong sense of trust and respect. More interestingly, the reason provided is always identical: She is authentic.

Within organizations, leader authenticity is a key factor in instilling trust and psychological safety. Doing so empowers individuals to perform at their highest capabilities. When team members feel safe at work, it's easier for them to participate in a team meeting, solve problems, collaborate on projects, and engage with their customers and peers. Authenticity creates a work culture where people feel more in tune and connected to their work community. This connectedness promotes loyalty to the organization and its purpose, attracting and retaining people who do their best work.

Whether at work or home, authentic living generates confidence, positivity, trust, and connectedness. These positive effects inherently set the stage for holding strong to what you believe in and what you hope to bring forth in your own life.

Chapter 8
Connect to a Greater Mission

||||||||||||||||||||||

Many great thinkers of our time have drawn the connection between self-discovery and greater purpose. Having a deep connection to your purpose—your why—propels you toward your goals while also rooting your actions in those values you hold most high. Gaining a clear line of sight into an authentic, values-based purpose aids in real-time, evidence-based decision-making. It also feels pretty good to live in alignment.

Having a purpose—an ultimate aim—is a shared human experience. While your purpose or desired end state may vary greatly from others, being driven by a deeper purpose is something we all share. Recognizing this commonality is important for two reasons:

1. Your unique talents are a critical cog in the larger system.

When we understand that all humans are driven by a mission, we better understand our role within the system. All individuals are part of an overarching dynamic, each with our own unique gifts to bring forward. Without the farmer, the cook wouldn't have raw ingredients to turn into delectable dishes. Without the coach, players wouldn't have the strategy to win the game. With-out the office manager, partners wouldn't have the organization and back-office support to serve key clients. We need people who are great at paralegal, those who can run large marketing organiza-tions, the leaders, the followers, the innovators, the caretakers, the rebels. This is how we survive, working together as a community to meet diverse needs. It is the very essence of how we move for-ward as a productive society.

Being acutely aware of the meaning, the intention, the moti-vating force behind our actions gives us the opportunity to focus our energies and efforts. Focused energy and effort lead to stronger results in shorter time frames.

Associating with a greater mission also boosts our mental well-being. Having a purpose in life—whether building widgets or sail-ing or volunteer work—affects your health. Purpose has even been shown to be more important for decreasing the risk of death than exercising regularly.

Researchers analyzed data from nearly seven thousand Amer-ican adults between the ages of 51 and 61. According to the study, published in the Journal of American Medicine, partici-pants without a strong life purpose were more than twice as likely to die compared with those who had one. "Just like people have basic physical needs, like to sleep and eat and drink, they have basic psychological needs," says Alan Rozanski, a professor at the Icahn School of Medicine at Mount Sinai. "The need for meaning and purpose is No. 1," Rozanski adds. "It's the deepest driver of well-being there is."[27]

2. Your ability and desire to pursue your purpose inher-ently support others to do the same.

Your choice to seek out your spark and bring it forth into the world matters. Owning and living your purpose can inspire greatness in those around you. This can occur in direct ways or in indirect ways, such as a female boss inspiring a young junior female employee, a kind stranger paying for the next person in line, a powerful speaker motivating an audience of juvenile offenders. We are inspired by those around us shining bright. They serve as a reminder of what is possible. And you—yes, you—have the power to provide that light for others.

AUTHOR SPOTLIGHT

The process of identifying my purpose—and thereby my company's greater mission—was messy, but fun.

You've probably noticed by now that I am a linear thinker which means that I tend toward analytic, methodic style of reasoning. Linear thinkers use information they have learned from one situation to apply it to another situation in order to solve problems, using patterns and formulas to make decisions in life. When I began the introspection that led to my purpose, I pulled upon a goal setting exercise I had first performed in graduate school.

The exercise begins with allowing yourself five minutes to brainstorm things you would like to accomplish. Each goal is then written onto a different sticky note, compiling as many as you are able to in the allotted time. In this instance, rather than writing aspirations, I used each small piece of paper to reflect aspects of work that I enjoyed. I brainstormed my favorite projects, attributes of bosses I admired, proudest moments, and positive feedback I had received over the years.

Once completed, I reviewed the pile of notes and tried to identify any themes or trends I could see. I hung large flip charts on the walls of my kitchen and hallway and began to organize the ideas in any way that made sense to me. As categories began to emerge, I would document broader ideas on the flip chart in marker. After several days of contemplating, coming back to review, and adding new thoughts, the charts formed a map of sorts.

There, staring back at me, was a collection of my strengths and talents. Coupled with my values, the categories of work became a blueprint for my business.

In 2009, Simon Sinek started a movement to help people become more inspired at work, and subsequently, inspire their colleagues and customers. His observations, explored in the book *Start with Why*, detail patterns in how powerful leaders think, act, and communicate.[28] He postulates that managers have the capacity to inspire cooperation, trust, and change by offering a clear connection to the core purpose behind the work, and by allowing the executors of the action to understand and connect with the meaning that led to said action.

This concept applies beyond teams to an organizational level as well. According to Deloitte's 2021 Global Human Capital Trends report, "purpose grounds organizations in a set of values that do not depend on circumstance. Those values, which sit at the intersection of economic, social, and human interest, serve as a benchmark against which actions and decisions can be weighed." It is not enough for leaders alone to be familiar with the strategy. They must explain the strategy and, critically, the why behind the strategy.[29]

Connecting to your primary values leads to authentic living. Authentic living helps bring forth your truest intentions—a living legacy of sorts. This legacy can be viewed as a personal mission that extends beyond any self-serving premise. Having a greater mission is important on an individual level, but also contributes to the greater good of the communities in which you participate.

So…*what is your living legacy?* Before we work together to narrow it down, consider how much attention you've given to determining your mission in the past:

Do you feel connected to something deeper than yourself?

How much time have you spent identifying what impact you hope to make on the world?

Have you ever considered what you want your legacy to be?

Zeroing in on your great mission in life can't be done in a day. If this is the first time you've contemplated what that noble purpose may be, go easy on yourself. It may take several iterations or reflection over a course of time to get down to specifics. Start with the goal of adding clarification to what you know today and progress from there.

Chapter 9

Identify Your Why

||||||||||||||||||||||||

Our realized purpose is important, impactful, and we alone are uniquely qualified to fulfill it. So how do we find it?

Taking our work on values to the next level, remember that your fundamental beliefs and principles drive your purpose. Whether you are an entrepreneur with the next big idea or a young adventurer seeking your next move, your *why* is the one constant that will guide you toward fulfillment in your work and life.

CLIENT SPOTLIGHT

One memorable client came to me on the edge of a breakdown. Sarah had been in the throes of a very toxic work environment for nearly ten years. The belittling behavior of supervisors had worn down her self-esteem, leaving her consumed with negativity. We worked together to identify the desired state, shifting her focus on the type of work and environment she did aspire to as opposed to focusing only on what she didn't like.

Our conversations began by discussing the tasks Sarah enjoyed most and the places she liked to perform those tasks. Through genuine curiosity, my question moved to focus on the adjectives that best described Sarah when she was operating *in the zone* (i.e., quick, focused progress is made on actions and energy levels are high). We also discussed the attributes she admired about herself and others, including those Sarah aspired to embody in the future. Lastly, the dialogue advanced to examining what she found most fulfilling about her work (i.e., the tasks, services, and/or products) and what impact she was hoping to make as a result of her efforts.

By following her values and natural inclinations, Sarah slowly found the confidence to formulate an ideal state— to understand who she wanted to be—and allow that to propel her decisions. Ultimately, she was able to step out of that toxic environment, and into her dream job that, as Sarah puts it, "is the position for which I've spent my entire life preparing."

Sarah could have easily blamed other people for her lack of ambition. She could have blamed others for her lack of confidence. Instead, Sarah put her energy into the meaningful purpose behind her work and that focus compelled her to new heights. Sarah's deeper desire to leave a professional legacy of creating calm out of chaos served as a guiding light, coaching and cheering her on in her moments of despair.

Born from strength

Evidence of your purpose is all around, often staring you in the face. Or perhaps ringing in your ears. The unofficial desig-

nations we take on and the functions we perform almost unconsciously are indicators of our spirit. What we are drawn to is not
an accident. Things that come naturally for us may signal another
level of purpose not yet discovered.

What formal and informal titles do you respond to?

- Confidante
- Fixer
- Challenger

Which tasks do you most enjoy?

- Strategy
- Relationship building
- Problem solving

What are you doing when you get lost "in the zone"?

- Dreaming
- Planning
- Working

When talking with others about your daily activities, listen for
a change in your voice. When your speech quickens, your conversation runs long, or you notice your determination to communicate insistently about the value of a topic, you are on the trail of a
passion. Think of that passion as a proxy for potential.

If you are passionate about helping others or making an
impact, dig deeper into these amiable interests:

How do you want to help others?

What does help mean to you?

If you wish to make an impact, try and get down to brass tacks
as to how you will know you've reached success:

Will the company make more money?

*Will the next generation be more equipped to handle life's ups and
downs?*

These nuances matter as they can serve as breadcrumbs leading to your realized purpose.

The way we spend our time is not an accident. Our lives are made up of days and our days are made up of a series of tasks. Tasks are typically a strong indicator of our purpose. Some professionals enter sales because they love to build relationships, others because of a knack for solving problems. Engineers may step into automation because they thrive on analyzing data while others love to see products come together from start to finish. When putting together a meal or planning a social event, do you find yourself getting lost in the details or eager to reach out and coordinate resources? Even when two people share the same role, they perceive that role differently. They prioritize differently, focusing on diverse elements of the task at hand.

Born from struggle

A considerable amount of people derives their greater mission from a particular challenge they faced or a trauma they endured. Once you arrive at a good understanding of your character and competencies, you are also more likely to view limitations and setbacks as opportunities. The American Psychological Association notes that career paths are often formed from this very concept. In exploring different professional pursuits, individuals often unconsciously opt to "actively master what they have suffered."[30]

Danielle recalls that when she graduated, she aspired to move into a creative field. While her academic experience had been stellar, placement resources were more geared towards business students. She wanted an advisor who had insight into and resources for the areas in which she had the most interest. Today, she provides those resources to others. Serving as a career director on a college campus, she ensures students have equitable networks and resources, regardless of their desired industry.

Trauma can be a trigger for developing a deeper mission. The media covers countless stories of survivors of abuse and neglect finding purpose in their pain. From volunteering on the weekends at a suicide hotline to funding vocational education for underserved communities, we are often inspired by and act on our greatest hardships.

It is better to light a candle than to curse the darkness.
—Eleanor Roosevelt

Empower and motivate

Consider how bringing purpose to the forefront of your mind can empower alignment in decisions and actions and make your current state of being more sustainable. Knowing where to place your energy allows for a more reasonable pace of work, narrowed project scopes, and firmer boundaries.

Your purpose—your *why*—can do the same. It will whisper to you when you fall down. It will call to you when you've stepped out of alignment. It will keep you warm on a cold night. Your why will help to crystallize the vision that will motivate you to the finish line.

Any self-discovery you make can be used for the purpose of greater alignment and impact. We'll talk more about mindset in future chapters but think for now how you might take knowledge about yourself and utilize it in your everyday life. If you value harmony and connection, you might apply these principles to your relationships and set a goal to schedule a routine date night with your partner. If you value relationship building and working with new technology, you may conduct an internet search to learn about various job roles that blend these two elements. If you value generosity and flexibility, you may set a goal in life to find a non-profit board that allows you to volunteer remotely.

Whether born out of our strengths or our struggles, finding your realized purpose always starts from within. I do a lot of work in support of full-grown adults figuring out what they want to be when they grow up. Whether they are contemplating a second career, wanting to flex their entrepreneurial muscle and start a business, or a stay-at-home parent looking to return to the workforce, the process is always grounded in clarification of values and objectives. Discover who you truly are and fully give every aspect of your uniqueness to the world.

Visit therequisitecourage.com/bonusmaterials to download an exercise to help explore your realized purpose.

Chapter 10

Fear of the Unknown

||||||||||||||||||||||||

As you enter into this work, particularly in the exercises ahead, it's normal to be apprehensive of unfamiliar territory. Most clients and audience members I have encountered over the years cite lack of certainty as a major roadblock on the road to pursuing their dreams. Have you ever asked yourself:

What if it doesn't work?

What if I go bankrupt?

What if I never meet anyone again?

This fear (and the fear of change overall) is not a result of the uncertainty that surrounds us but is generated from a lack of clarity within us. Consider: nothing is certain. We live every single moment of every day with a total lack of certainty—no guarantee of what will come forward from one minute to the next.

Promoted by cultural norms in today's society, our natural inclination is to obsess over what we cannot control. Consider instead, it is the high quantity of variables that cause us a heightened level of discomfort. As we reduce these variables by focusing in on who we are and what we want, we can more confidently step into the unknown.

Choose the right response

Responding to change with a fear response is to obsess over what you cannot control. Reacting to change with a conquer response is to focus on what you can control. Namely, your values and purpose. While you may not know what's going to happen, choosing a conquer response over a fear-based response can help you know that you're headed in the right direction.

Lose your job?

Fear response: What's going to happen to me? Am I going to be able to pay my mortgage? Will I be able to get health insurance and take care of my sick child?

Conquer response: What roles will I apply for? Which companies do I want to target? What resources will I call upon to help update my resume and learn to leverage LinkedIn?

Suddenly, in this situation, the variables become more manageable and less scary because now you have more clarity, not certainty.

Preparing to move across the country?

Fear response: What will happen if I leave my family? Am I going to be able to make new friends in a new city? How will I know where I'm going?

Conquer response: What is my objective for making the move? What aspects of life will I be closer to/goals I can achieve in my new location? How will this relocation help me live more authentically?

Responding to conquer-based queries shifts focus away from the irrational and uncontrollable to what is known and manageable.

Launching a new initiative?

Fear response: What if it doesn't work? Am I risking my financial well-being? Will my spouse/boss/partner/children think I'm a failure?

Conquer response: What learning can I expect from this experience? What factors can I manage to aid in success? Who in my support system will I call upon for encouragement and endorsement? How can I celebrate making it this far?

Certainty is being secure in what is going to happen next. It is sequential and knowledge based. To have certainty, you must have control over every aspect of a situation. That is just not how life works. Clarity, on the other hand, is about focusing on what you can control. No matter what happens, you're still living your values and pursuing your realized purpose.

It was a clarity of vision—the outline of a desirable end game—that helped bring me through my high school trauma and so many fearful moments thereafter. Each time, courage has come only after I gained clarity—around my strengths, my values, my driving purpose. You can live with clarity and courage, too. Build upon your foundational values and gain momentum from your realized purpose.

Courage in Action

Make a Values Connection

Knowing what we hold dear in this world is essential to stepping through fear and into courageous change. It provides the clarity to build a plan of action for navigating our life and career and tackling roadblocks along the way.

Recall the work you did in the **Setting Your Intention Courage in Action**. Write your desired area of change from that exercise below. Keep it front of mind as you complete the next activities.

_____

Change You Desire
Ex. new job in new city

How might identifying your unique strengths and values affect the area of your life you desire to change? List your top-ranked values from Chapter 6 below. Next to each value, write down a few thoughts on how this particular value aligns with and supports your desired change.

VALUE	CHANGE PHRASES
Ex. Independence	Moving to a new city will force me to stand on my own two feet.
	I will have the chance to practice self-governance once living on my own.
	I will prove my self-sufficiency to myself and others by acclimating to the new environment.
	The paycheck from my new role will reduce my reliance on family for financial support.
Ex. _____	_____
	_____
	_____
	_____
Ex. _____	_____
	_____
	_____
	_____
Ex. _____	_____
	_____
	_____
	_____
Ex. _____	_____
	_____
	_____
	_____

Ask the Five Whys to Explore Your Life's Purpose

The Five Whys is an iterative interrogative technique used to explore the cause-and-effect relationships underlying a particular problem. Typically, the method is used to determine the root cause of a defect or problem by repeating the question, "Why?" Each answer forms the basis of the next question.

Here, you will use the Five Whys to further explore your life's purpose.

Begin by writing down a general purpose statement. Ask yourself: **What is your living legacy? If you could have just one impact on the world, what would it be?**

Ex. I would like to help others.

_____

_____

Read your response immediately above and ask yourself: **why?**
Ex. I want to give back in the same way others helped me.

_____

_____

Read your response immediately above and ask yourself: **why?**
Ex. I would like to make a positive difference in someone's life at a time they are struggling.

_____

_____

Read your response immediately above and ask yourself: **why?**
Ex. A mentor supported me through a difficult time when I was younger, and it completely changed my life. I want to do that for someone else.

_____

_____

Read your response immediately above and ask yourself: **why?**
Ex. Impacting a child's life at a critical age would allow me to tap into my purpose and feel fulfilled.

_____

_____

Read your response immediately above and ask yourself: **why?**
Ex. Returning that goodness to the universe would help me feel as though I am using my trauma to create good in the world.

_____

_____

Your values define who you are.

Your purpose statement describes what you stand for. Write it below.

Ex. I create goodness in the world by using the trauma I've experienced to help others.

_____

_____

_____

_____

You are now able to dive into the second step of accessing the requisite courage with a clear understanding of who you are and what you stand for. This level of clarity is crucial as we begin to assess your alignment to these values and focus on the aspects of life that will serve that purpose.

Part 3:

Conviction

c on·vic·tion* | *kən- ˈvik-shən

noun: the quality of showing that one is firmly convinced
of what one believes or says

Chapter 11
That Which Follows

||||||||||||||||||||||

I looked in the mirror. My thirty-one-year-old eyes were bloodshot and my face puffy from crying. A close friend and confidante was waiting back at the table sipping on a five-dollar margarita. She had demonstrated the patience of a saint over the last three hours as I painfully recounted the latest discovery of deceit. I poured over the details of one plan after another of how I would tell my husband I was finally going to leave him.

There, in the Applebee's bathroom, I looked in the mirror and saw a flash of courage behind my glossed-over eyes. There, I decided once and for all that enough was enough. I was ready to burn the plan. I had known what needed to happen for years now but had been waiting for the right time. The right time in this marriage. The right time in this life. The right time to own my values over my identity. The moment to break free from the perfect image I had manufactured to distract from the imperfection within. The time was now—my confidence had finally caught up with my clarity.

> I have often heard them referred to as defining events. A distinct moment in time where you become acutely aware that everything that came before would be distinctly different than that which follows.

I ran past the table with determination, grabbed my purse, and thanked my friend as I ran out the door. I drove home, defiant of the speed limit signs I could barely make out through the tears streaming down my face. I came into the house, checked in on my sleeping babies (two-year-old Claire and six-week-old Matt), and moved to the bedroom.

"Get up," I said.

He stirred.

"We need to talk."

The evening wore on as we sparred back and forth regarding the minute details of it all. As if the exact day or lunch location changed the overarching fact that my husband—the father of my children—had been leading a double life since the day we met. He tried to keep the conversation moving in hopes of delaying the inevitable. But after years of denying my inner voice in support of my outer image, I was done. It was time to walk away from the custom-built home and picture-perfect family.

The next morning, we crossed paths and my husband made an all-too-common plea for sympathy. It was too late. I had already released the guilt I had been carrying for his wrongdoings. My focus was on reconnecting to my authentic self. A prediction appeared in my mind and quickly formed into words that flew out of my mouth without warning. It wasn't a response; it was a promise. It wasn't for him; it was for me. An affirmation: "Today and every day hereafter, my life is going to get better."

Light the way

To survive this mess and manifest my prediction, I had to let go of the plan I had been chasing for all those years. My certainty came from knowing not only had I taken a stand against his egregious acts, but I had finally taken a stand for the imperfect me. The woman who had set out on a path nearly a decade earlier was now ready to say to herself, her kids, the world, "Hey, I'm on the wrong path. This one didn't lead where I was so sure it would. I have to start over."

The night before, glaring into that mirror, I had realized that as long as I clung to the concept of perfection, I was robbing myself of the beauty and bounty of imperfection. I began to finally let go of predictability in hopes of finding possibility.

We must be willing to let go of the life we planned
so as to have the life that is waiting for us.
—Joseph Campbell

Living with fearless authenticity requires letting go of that which does not serve you and embracing what does. Courage can't be had without the unwavering assurance that you have done the work to be ready. Recognize that the paralyzing aspect of disruption stems from resistance. Trust that a purpose built on values allows for pivot as needed. This applies to external sources like hurricanes or job loss; and self-induced change like starting a business or leaving a marriage.

Rest and reset in knowing that while the plan may have changed, your deeper purpose need not.

As Gandhi once stated, "Your values become your destiny." Even when we have clarified our values and can point to the space we are headed—visualizing the finish line and all the rewards and accolades that come with it—sometimes we simply don't have the confidence to take the first step.

Courage requires that you attach conviction to your realized purpose to fuel confidence. Employ a growth mindset and allow the ambient glow of smoldering ashes to light the way to new possibilities. From here, we find the momentum to step into action.

Chapter 12
Burn the Plan

||||||||||||||||||||||||

In the chaos of day-to-day life, planning has become a necessity. Whether you're a busy parent or the CEO of a Fortune 100, getting yourself (and your pack) from point A to B requires a rigid and risk-averse plan. Plans are important; they save time and—when variables (and ducks) are all in a row—solid plans support smooth execution.

Even if you don't consider yourself a big planner, planning is still a natural part of the way we go through life. Preschool teachers showcase visual aids to let children know the day's order of events. Meetings of the PTA and the National Association of Sales Professionals alike begin with a shared agenda outlining timeframes and topics. Investment advisors make life-long careers out of helping people manage their wealth to plan for retirement. As humans, we feel most at ease when we know what is happening next.

RESEARCH SPOTLIGHT

The planning skill is central to all human behavior. Defined as formulating an organized method for action in advance, planning behaviors have many pragmatic benefits.

Michael E. Bratman, the Abbie Birch Durfee Professor for the School of Humanities and Science at Stanford University, notes that planning is essential to people's sense of freedom and autonomy over their own lives. "Fitting together different plans in a coherent, consistent and stable way is part of what it means for humans to have unified thinking concerning what they are doing."[31]

In his recently published book, *Planning, Time, and Self-Governance*, Bratman explores how the human capacity for planning plays a central role in our propensity to act and think together and in our self-governance.

Moreover, in-depth studies conducted by E. J. Masicampo (Wake Forest University) and Roy Baumeister (Florida State and *Psychology Today* blogger) demonstrated that following a specific plan to achieve a desired goal actually opens cognitive resources to be available for our other projects.[32] Planning then inherently helps us to not only be successful with the goal at hand, but allows time for pursuing other objectives as well. As soon as the plan is developed, our minds can release full attention from one goal and start contemplating others.

The necessity for planning to bring thoughts and teams together in pursuit of a common goal is undeniable. Given the benefits, it's easy to understand our natural inclination to formulate and predict what's needed before going into action.

Given our reliance on planning and the upfront investment we put in, it can take some time to recognize when a plan goes awry. Some signs that we are off-track are easier to notice than others.

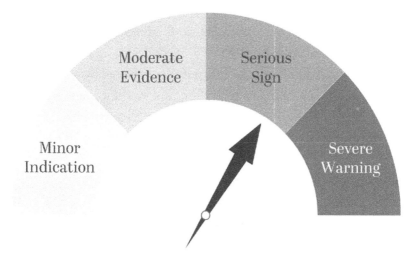

Minor indication: The meeting closes in ten minutes, and the team hasn't finished discussing the second half of the agenda.

Moderate evidence: Kathy is a devoted mother of four children and volunteers her free time to serve on the city council. As her youngest enters preschool, she finds herself feeling restless and looking for more ways to serve the community while still having the flexibility to support her family as needed.

Serious sign: Barbara has been groomed for decades to take over the family business. As her father prepares for retirement at the end of this year, her thoughts are wrought with questions around whether she wants to spend the rest of her career in manufacturing. She is losing sleep and, as a result, lacking focus and motivation around the office.

Severe warning: Jim is feeling restless as he enters his fourth year as a project coordinator with a local paint supplier. He is burned out from late nights away from his family and there appear to be no opportunities for advancement. The bills are piling up and the stress is beginning to affect his health.

Feeling unsettled or unsatisfied is a common indicator that your life may be out of alignment. That your plan is no longer serving your needs or supporting your values. Other indicators may include feedback from a loved one (such as an intervention) or a simple lack of momentum. Whether prompted by a large void or a small crack in the clay, when you find yourself spending time and energy toward an identity that does not serve you, it's time for a change.

Learning to let go

Willfully disengaging from a part of your life—be it a geographic location, another human being, firmly held belief, or a whim for a future that is no longer—can be tough. Remember when we talked about how easy it is to maintain the status quo in Chapter 10? Your natural inclination toward safety and comfort will kick in when tested with the fire of uncertainty. Your mind may start to rationalize the signs of misalignment you so carefully noticed in an attempt to convince you to dismiss or deny the need for change. But you must hold steady.

You may prefer the slow and low churn of a phased approach to transition. You may wish to light a match and allow your prior plan to go up in smoke. Whatever the approach, deciding to shift away from the original course of action can be both cathartic and stressful. Make a decision and hold to it. Where possible, create physical distance between you and the aspect of life you need to relinquish. Take comfort in regaining the mind space that had been directed at undeserving actions. Practice forgiveness.

Clarity—awareness and understanding of who you are and what you stand for—is the basis for those decisions. If you value stability and security, taking a giant leap to quit your job without a known source of income would not be a good way to initiate change. If you value power and accountability, positioning yourself as a change agent may serve as a great motivator. Get into the habit of checking back into your values and purpose as you move through decision-making. They serve as a good foundation upon which to find a plan (and identity) that does serve you.

Holding on is believing that there's only a past;
letting go is knowing that there's a future.
—Daphne Rose Kingma

Time to grieve

Change inherently requires a simultaneous letting go and picking up. Loss and gain. There is a loss associated with any significant shift in our lives—an erosion of predictability, identity, trust. Sometimes change demands cultural, ethnic, or spiritual sacrifices. Conviction is born from acknowledging that void and allotting the time to grieve. Then, when ready, sift through the ashes to label what ideas, concepts, and beliefs can be salvaged. Decidedly let the rest go.

A key factor after experiencing disruption is to grant yourself the permission you need to grieve. Recall the stages Tanya faced in Chapter 5. Her job loss triggered denial, anger, bargaining, and depression before inviting acceptance back into her thinking. The process is neither linear nor swift.

When facing my divorce, admitting that I needed a new plan felt like an acknowledgment that I had done something wrong. Maybe I had made poor decisions, and I wasn't so perfect after all. From that point on, I could not carry on as a "flawless decision-maker," "the girl with a perfect plan," or "the one with it all together." I needed to accept I was still a whole person despite the misstep.

Running back to what is safe. Running back to what came before the disruption. This is tempting for all of us. A key component of conviction is to define what was before and what will be after.

Grapple with the loss for as long and intensely as you need to. All the while with the trust that when you are done, you never have to go through it again. Grieve your plan. Your perfect decisions. Your puzzle that is just missing one piece. Be willing to sit with pain. Be brave enough to do nothing. See the battle for what it is. See the blank canvas in front of you for what it could be.

Visit therequisitecourage.com/bonusmaterials to download an exercise that pinpoints the things in your life that you have been holding onto for too long.

Chapter 13
Fear of Inadequacy

||||||||||||||||||||||

Let's be honest—we tell ourselves horrible things. No matter the level of success obtained, accomplishments achieved, awards garnered, our minds attempt to convince us it is all a mirage. We are convinced that our success is a mere accident and that we lack the expertise/talent/strength required to achieve—and maintain—our place in life. Feeling like an impostor, we worry that we will be exposed as a fraud at any moment.

Impostor phenomenon is a term coined in 1978 by clinical psychologists Dr. Pauline Rose Clance and colleague Dr. Suzanne Imes and is thought to affect nearly seventy percent of current-day Americans.[33] Clance observed a psychological pattern among group therapy patients wherein an individual doubts their skills, talents, or accomplishments and has a persistent internalized fear of being exposed as a fraud. This pattern persists despite external evidence to the contrary: scoring well on standardized tests, earning advanced degrees, and receiving professional awards.

As an executive coach for more than ten years, I can confidently state that I have not encountered a single client who didn't suffer from this unfounded yet very real fear of inadequacy. In fact, research suggests the more successful we are, the more likely we are to suffer from this debilitating thought process.

CLIENT SPOTLIGHT

A client came to me with aspirations of being a professional speaker. Shawn had been on the circuit for almost a year, an active member of the National Speaker Association, and a respected thought leader. To the world, he was a speaker. To himself, he wanted to be a speaker. We spent time talking through his own definition of speaker. Shawn realized he was trying to play a game, follow the rules, do what everyone else was suggesting without trusting in the path he had already set. He started to own his positioning. Stopped telling others he was on his way to becoming a speaker and would introduce himself as a professional speaker. He focused on improving his positioning as opposed to trying to earn his position.

When you feel unworthy and ill-equipped, you frequently disregard any evidence provided to the contrary. The tendency to personalize failure and globalize success is an outstanding example of how this syndrome burrows its way into our consciousness.

"I couldn't reach that milestone because I wasn't organized enough."

"We would have never made it to the deadline without the support of the entire team."

"I was too scared to move forward, therefore my partner had to do all the hard work."

"We are excited about the new house, I'm so lucky to have a husband that is so successful."

The propensity for dismissing your accomplishments can be hidden under the premise of being humble, but the fear of inadequacy goes far beyond that. When you are unable to accept a compliment without immediately explaining the external forces that led to your success, it's more fear than virtue.

Pairing with perfectionism

The impostor phenomenon and perfectionism (explored in more detail in Chapter 7) often go hand in hand. So-called impostors think every task they tackle must be done perfectly, and they rarely ask for help. This leads to two typical responses: An impostor may procrastinate, putting off an assignment out of fear that he or she won't be able to complete it to the necessary high standards. Or they may over-prepare, spending much more time on a task than is necessary.

Impostor workaholics are addicted to the validation that comes from working, not to the work itself. The key to getting past it, experts say, is making accurate, realistic assessments of your performance. Start training yourself to veer away from external validation. No one should have more power to make you feel good about yourself than you—even your boss when they give your project the stamp of approval. On the flip side, learn to take constructive criticism seriously, not personally. As you become more attuned to internal validation and able to nurture your inner confidence that states you're competent and skilled, you'll be able to ease off the gas as you gauge how much work is reasonable.

I attended a global conference several years ago wherein I received a vital piece of advice. An industry colleague and illustrious entrepreneur pulled me aside and whispered, "Don't try so hard." When I looked back with confusion, she continued by reaffirming, "This is who you are. Trust it." Success is not what you do, it is who you are. Achievement and alignment will come naturally if you just allow it to be. I have found since incorporating her counsel that trusting my station removes the high-intensity pressure to always do, do, do.

Think back to those impostor statements. Here is what personalizing success and owning your power can sound like:

"I gave it my best effort and I have a lot to be proud of."

"My hard work and dedication helped the group reach our goal."

"I contributed my fair share and let my partner know where I was facing limitations so that we could each apply our talents to cross the finish line together."

"We are excited about the new house. My husband and I have worked hard and made good choices to support living the life we want."

Start telling yourself honorable things.

Chapter 14

Set Your Mind

||||||||||||||||||||||

Personal growth is predicated on self-talk that champions, rather than sabotages, your efforts. Our mindset—the perspective we hold for the things that occur around us and to us—is the driving force behind our ability to focus on what is most important and true. As such, mindset is the key to cementing your conviction.

Psychologist Carol Dweck offers a compelling look at two distinct mindsets, fixed versus growth, and their subsequent effect on our behavior. A fixed mindset is set on the belief that you are born with a pre-determined and somewhat static set of aptitudes, interests, or temperaments. Often based on childhood experiences, a fixed mindset can appear to offer control and reward. Following the belief that everyone contains a predetermined set of talents, children are encouraged to apply those skills, reap the positive results of good performance. Essentially, it provided a formula for self-esteem and a path to love and respect from others.

RESEARCH SPOTLIGHT[34]

Dweck's popular TED talk, "The Power of Believing That You Can Improve," outlines how operating in a space just outside of your comfort zone is the key to improving performance. A critical element to deliberate practice, it is best to strive for improvement in a way that stretches the ability as opposed to simply repeating a task again and again without awareness or attention.

Dweck shares an anecdote wherein she learned of a high school in Chicago where students had to pass a certain number of courses to graduate. If they didn't pass a course, Dweck explains, they got the grade "Not Yet." She celebrated what an effective means of reminding students they are on a learning curve. While a failing grade precipitates feelings of going nowhere, "Not Yet" gives one a path into the future.

How we word things affects confidence. When we recognize that pushing our own limits toward something new and different creates new neural pathways in the brain, we are reminded that intelligence is not fixed. When we change the terminology we use to describe our improvement efforts, we are reminded that success is within reach.

What has served us in the past may not always serve us in the present. On a subconscious level, we are constantly monitoring and interpreting what happens around us, processing what occurrences mean and what we should do as a result. It's how we stay on track. But sometimes the translation goes awry, and we place more extreme interpretations on things that happen:

"If I have yet to succeed in my area of interest, I must not have what it takes."

"Once a failure, always a failure."

"I was never very smart, I'm not capable of doing more than the status quo."

This thinking results in exaggerated feelings of anxiety, depression, anger, or superiority and is contrasted by a growth mindset. A growth mindset is based on the belief that your basic qualities are things that you can cultivate through your efforts. With a growth mindset, intelligence and personality are malleable and we acknowledge everyone can change and grow through application and experience.

"I continue to learn and grow every day, unleashing more of my potential with each action."

"Failure is a good indicator that I am willing to push my comfort zone and try new things to expand my skill set."

"I have unlimited potential and can only be restrained by an unwillingness to try."

FIXED MINDSET	GROWTH MINDSET
Avoid challenges.	Embraces challenges.
Talent is innate.	Talent can be developed.
Gives up easily.	Effort leads to success.
Failure is proof of limits.	Failure is growth.

When we shift our focus to embracing an ongoing development model there is very little that can stop us. Psychologist and author Dr. Barbara Markway says, "Paradoxically, by being more willing to fail, you'll actually succeed more—because you're not waiting for everything to be 100 percent perfect before you act. Taking more shots will mean making more of them."[35] As theoretical shots are made, confidence in ourselves and our abilities grows.

Where confidence begins

Despite it being for many the holy grail of positive mental health, self-confidence starts with a simple decision to incorporate a learning approach in your life. Trust that you will succeed and if you fail, you will learn along the way. The desire to learn with or without accompanying success increases the number of chances you take. Statically, more attempts increase the likelihood of a positive result. The more positive results you experience, the greater your level of confidence. The approach quickly becomes cyclical wherein high self-confidence allows for self-trust which, in turn, grants you permission to try harder things.

But if effort can lead to such great things, why is it so terrifying?

Ah, the crux of fear for the high achiever. One reason we shy away from effort is that, in the fixed mindset, great geniuses are not supposed to need it. So just needing it casts a shadow on your ability. In other words, if we have to work hard at something, we assume we must be bad at it. If I have to try multiple posts to gain followers, I must not be cut out to be an influencer. If I cannot deliver this sales pitch the right way the first time, I must not understand my product. If I have to study night and day to pass the exam, I must not have a natural talent for this line of work.

The second reason is that it robs you of all your excuses. Without effort, you can always say, "I could have been (fill in the blank)." But once you step out to try, you can't say that anymore. If I never get on stage, I can tell myself I could have been a world-renowned speaker. If I never go to New York, I can convince myself I could have made it on Broadway. If I never move away from home, I can perpetuate the belief that I could have been a world traveler. When we put our energy and intellect into a single dream—go all in—and that dream doesn't come to fruition, the resulting disappointment can be a nightmare.

So you stay in your full-time job, griping about the pitfalls of Corporate America and postulating how successful you could be if given the opportunity to break out on your own. This feels safer. Quitting your job and opening a small business brings inevitable failure (and there will be lots along the way) to the front and center. You are faced with stepping into and embracing the learning that failure brings with it, or else admit defeat.

Sometimes you just have to take the leap and
build your wings on the way down.
—Kobi Yamada

We will talk more about working with an experimental mindset in future chapters. For now, take time to explore the areas in your own life that have been prematurely shut down by a fixed mindset.

- An education
- A career path
- A committed relationship
- A dream project (book, song, side hustle)

Reflect for a moment on how remaining open to a growth mindset may support deeper conviction and ultimate pursuit of your goals. Now, let's train your brain to do just that.

Chapter 15

Train Your Brain

||||||||||||||||||||||

There is very little that can stop us when we believe in our own capabilities. We've already talked in previous chapters about why we need to identify our values and face the decisions that come with this knowledge. So how do we go from *know* to *ready to go*?

To train your brain to achieve a growth mindset, you simply need to break down everyday scenarios into events, beliefs, and consequences. Psychologist Albert Ellis asserted that, "People are not disturbed by things but rather by their view of things." He developed Rational Emotive Behavior Therapy (REBT) to help patients challenge dysfunctional beliefs and replace them with more sensible beliefs.[36] His framework breaks down the connection between an event that may serve as a trigger and the irrational evaluations that follow. When this methodology is taken to the next level—playing out the rational response—it can serve as an incredible tool for establishing and solidifying a growth mindset.

Breaking it down

The grid below is a visual diagram of the cognitive behavioral therapy concept proposed by Ellis. The framework serves as an excellent tool to walk through the steps in any scenario.

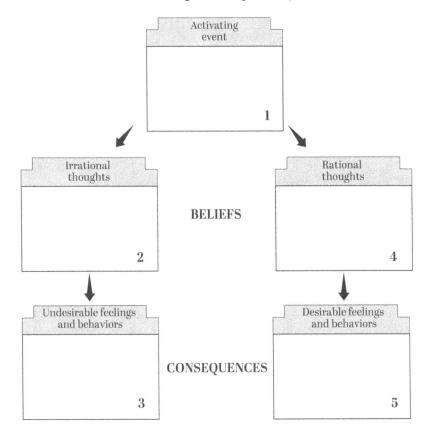

This approach allows us to work from a single "activating event" and walk through all the irrational beliefs and resulting emotions to then the rational beliefs and resulting behaviors and emotions. A powerful and quick way to stop negative thinking in its tracks.

Let's walk through an example together. You'll need a pen/ pencil; it helps to write it down as opposed to simply processing it in your mind. Our brains accept the written word as stronger facts than the thoughts that run through our heads.[37]

Think of a scenario that spiked a negative thought pattern. Summarize this activating event in a single sentence in box #1.

Moving to box #2, list the automatic self-based thoughts that flood your mind after recalling the event.

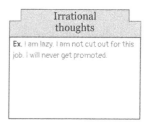
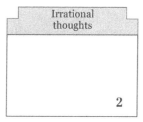

Now, using the space provided in box #3, note the undesirable feelings and behaviors that stem from the irrational thoughts presented in box #2.

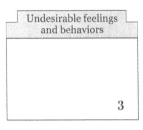

Let's return to the activating event and, this time, move to box #4 to contemplate some of the rational beliefs that might explain being late to work.

Rational thoughts

Ex. I worked late on that project last night. I am feeling overwhelmed by the competing priorities of a dotted-line reporting relationship. My body needed extra rest after the long week. I have established a strong reputation in my company and no one will judge.

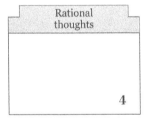

And finally, list the feelings and behaviors that result from these rational thoughts in box #5:

Desirable feelings and behaviors

Ex. Proud. Energized. Self-aware. Rested. Relieved. I can set up a meeting with my boss to discuss prioritizing my work differently. I manage myself and my actions well and deserve to take some extra time for myself as needed.

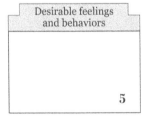

Visit therequisitecourage.com/bonusmaterials to download additional templates any time you are challenged with shifting your mindset from unworthy to unshaken.

Opportunity is all around

The examples offered are important because they show that we do have the ability to change our own perspective and provide our brains with the focus they need to act according to our purpose.

Another way to train your brain is through the frequency illusion. Also known as the Baader-Meinhof phenomenon, the frequency illusion is a cognitive bias in which, after noticing something for the first time, there is a tendency to notice it more often. The essence of fashion trends comes from this very principle: when you learn that Dr. Martens are back in vogue, suddenly you will notice everyone wearing them. This leads someone to believe that it has a high frequency. The illusion is caused by two cognitive processes: selective attention and confirmation bias. You see, your brain has an incredible talent for pattern recognition and, given that attention is a limited resource, will narrow in on the parameters you provide.[38]

Can you recall the last time you went shopping for a new car? Let's say it was a red Jeep Cherokee. Did you happen to notice there were a great deal more red Cherokees on your drive home? Of course you did. The act of selecting your car made this particular make, model, and color a focal point in your mind, prompting your brain to take note of the repeated pattern.

This straightforward principle demonstrates how quickly your brain will move in a suggested direction and how it can work in your favor to highlight what you dictate is important. Using this to your advantage, you can begin to zero in on patterns, opportunities, and thoughts that drive you toward courage instead of away from it. Reclaim your brain for courageous action by doing this work. Our brains are amazing machines. In addition to recognizing patterns, the human brain loves questions too.

Powerful questions

Let's explore how you can focus your mind on what serves you with the use of intentional questions. Take a walk down memory lane with me. Think about your first kiss. Carefully recall your surroundings, your smattering of emotions, and your partner.

Now answer this:

What color was the house you grew up in?

Notice how quickly your brain moved its attention to your childhood home. Despite being ingrained in a detailed, emotion-heavy memory as significant as your first kiss, your brain shifted gears in an instant. This is not simply because you are good at following directions. Questions trigger a mental reflex known as "instinctive elaboration" wherein any question posed immediately highjacks the thought process to focus in on searching for an answer.[39]

Coupling this biological instinct with selective attention, you can take the Baader-Meinhof phenomenon to the next level. Likely, you are already asking your subconscious mind a variety of not-so-positive questions. From the moment the alarm goes off until you settle into your desk, you are engaged in ongoing speculation about the coming day. What if we turned that projecting up a notch?

Begin every day by giving your brain a challenge: a positive and intentional question that it can work to solve throughout the day. The benefit of such exercise is not only moving you toward your desired life but also mitigating negative thoughts.

Rather than asking, "What will my boss yell at me about today?" maybe the question becomes, "Where can I find success at work?"

Rather than wondering what you and your partner will argue about tonight, perhaps outline a purposeful question like, "What can I do to support my partner today?"

Rather than entering the day expecting things to go wrong or mistakes to be made, ask yourself "How can I embrace positivity today?" "How can I live courageously?" "How can I be my best self today?"

When faced with adversity, it can be hard to think of anything beyond getting away from the problem. This human default can be extremely detrimental. Our brains do not work in the negative. When you say, "My goal is to not be poor," the brain focuses its energy on the keyword: poor. Instead, one should say, "My goal is to reach financial independence." The brain then narrows in on financial independence, and again, begins to set the conditions for success.

Give yourself something worthwhile to chew on in your free time. Try flipping around the following worrisome mantras to create powerful questions instead:

Why do I keep failing at this?

Ex. Which step in the process do I need to study further and practice more often?

_____

_____

Where will I get the money for that?

_____

_____

What will go wrong today?

_____

_____

How will I explain this to them?

_____

_____

Visit therequisitecourage.com/bonusmaterials to download an exercise that helps you write a powerful anchor question to guide you through each day.

Focus on what matters

In October of 2000, the CEO of Starbucks, Orin C. Smith, announced an aggressive global expansion. "I believe that we have dramatically underestimated the size of the global market, including the number of points of distribution and the power of the Starbucks brand," Smith said. The coffeehouse chain kept its promise and, over the course of five years, grew from approximately five thousand stores to fifteen thousand.

Unfortunately, while locations grew, revenues shrank. The company expanded too quickly and drastically damaged its brand. When stock prices were cut in half, CEO Howard Schultz returned from an eight-year hiatus to reverse the curse. Schultz focused on bringing back the customer voice, ensuring quality products were placed in consumer hands with consistency. His extreme attention to patrons also led to the creation of a channel where customers could present their voices and views. As relationships with the customers strengthened, profits followed. Starbucks stands today as the world's largest coffee house chain and is considered at the forefront of the United States' second wave of coffee culture.[40]

Numerous leadership gurus before and after Schultz's corporate transformation have identified focus as the secret to high performance and fulfillment. Focused efforts lead to focused results. Working to reduce the variables around us allows our mind to hone in on what is truly important and make significant progress in that singular direction. The more progress we make, the more confident we are in our abilities to continue along the path to success. The action is reinforced and therefore more likely to be repeated.

Attention is arguably one of today's scarcest resources. We live in a fast-paced world where distractions abound. And Tony Robbins has famously said, "Energy flows where the attention goes."

RESEARCH SPOTLIGHT

In his recent best-selling book, *Focus*, psychologist and journalist Daniel Goleman persuasively argues that now more than ever we must learn to sharpen focus if we are to contend with, let alone thrive, in a complex world.[41]

We live in distracting times. Goleman asserts that the constant urge to respond to the overwhelming amount of information and stimuli in our environment leads us to a state of continuous partial attention in which we leap carelessly from one thing to another, from our phones to our email to Facebook. In doing so, we weaken our ability to select what we pay attention to.

The distractions that envelop us not only threaten to waste our time and reduce our productivity, but they also diminish our ability to immerse ourselves in the present. Selective attention is the key to high performance in a word of endless distractions. The stronger our ability to select what we focus on, the better we are at ignoring potential distractions.

Goleman notes that if we can develop our ability to ignore distractions and focus well, we can help to increase our performance, and enable ourselves to have more profound reflections and deeper insights. Practicing mindfulness, positive thinking and engaging in focused preparation are among the most recommended ways to enhance your level of attention.

To manifest change in your life, you need to focus on your destination, not your point of origin. In the case of Starbucks, Schultz found success identifying the problem and then turning all his attention to the solution—looking to the future and not the past. When you're dreading a tough task and expect it to be difficult and unpleasant, you may unconsciously set goals around what you don't want to happen rather than what you do want. But the change is not about running away from a dysfunctional marriage or a soul-sucking job. Rather, it's about reclaiming your life and standing up for your sense of self.

Positive, sustainable change requires a set objective and the confidence and commitment to run towards it. You are not abandoning your family to move across the country but heading towards a life and location that will feed your soul. You are not losing weight but embracing a healthy lifestyle. You are not quitting your job but getting ready to unleash your potential. Think in terms of approach versus avoidance. Talk to yourself and others about the positive outcome you want to achieve as opposed to the adverse result you are hoping to avoid.

Conviction is rooted in the idea that we are creating a reality for ourselves no matter what. The next step in resetting after a disruption involves sifting through the ashes. It's time to view what has been left behind and make some strategic decisions about what can be salvaged and what is better to leave in the rubble. Conviction may involve loss, yet you stand so much to gain. There is something very cathartic and refreshing about burning the plan. It's a personal (and sometimes public) acknowledgment that you are trading predictability and perfection in favor of authenticity and alignment.

The odds of recreating another tragic situation are too high when you are busy looking in the rearview mirror. Spend your time with your chin up, staring straight ahead. Keep your eyes and your heart on the positive outcome you so desperately deserve.

Chapter 16
Build an Abundance Mentality

|||||||||||||||||||||||||

We've demonstrated that there is no shortage of opportunities that surround us when we choose to set our thoughts on a given path. Often, these occurrences are passed off as mere coincidences. I prefer to acknowledge that we live in a world full of opportunities. Those red Jeeps from the last chapter didn't just show up because your mind beckoned them; they were there all along.

Whatever you're ready for is ready for you.
—Mark Victor Hansen

Time after time, I have seen examples of people manifesting opportunities within mere hours after setting their intention. A client who finally reaches out for some coaching after years at an abusive employer gets a job offer three days later. A colleague decides they are ready for a next-level strategic project and learns the next day of a pending acquisition. A new mom begins to put herself out there to make new friends in the district and receives an unexpected invitation to join a committee.

Be advised you don't need to sit back and wait for the universe to work in your favor. You have the power to beckon its abundance. You can build your abundance mentality right now. The next time you are feeling a lack, put the very thing you seek out into the universe. When you are feeling sick, try to emulate more compassion to those around you. When you are feeling lonely, think of people in your life who could benefit from a broader support system and reach out to them with open arms. Offering what we need most to the universe will send it right back like a boomerang.

When you need to be reminded of abundance, bring it forward: text a friend you haven't spoken to in a while, call to check in on your elders, offer gratitude to someone you wouldn't normally take the time to recognize. Your effort does not need to be immense for the impact to be immediate. The behaviors shift your mind's focus. Self-loathing transforms into feeling powerful. You become acutely aware of your ability to change the world, one small piece at a time.

Be the light

After the divorce was final, I wanted to surround my children with light to contrast all the darkness that had come into our home and lives. So I asked myself, day after day, "Where can I find the light?" At times, the universe would respond with a sunny afternoon wherein we could all take a walk and explore the neighborhood. In other instances, my subconscious would notice DIY craft ideas that would allow for quality time with the kids and result in some decor that brightened up our apartment.

My greatest inspiration came while I was confronting the reality of spending a birthday—celebrating my existence—as a middle-aged mom who was out of touch with her own reality.

I decided that if I couldn't find examples of light to show my children, we would need to create our own. The Birthday Mission was launched. I committed to performing one random act of kindness per year of my life. In what felt like a nod of support from the universe, the radio played, "This Little Light of Mine" when we got into the car the morning of our first outing.

This little light of mine
I'm going to let it shine
Oh, this little light of mine
I'm going to let it shine

Tears rolled down my face before we even left the driveway.

AUTHOR SPOTLIGHT

My first Birthday Mission was in 2012 and I took Claire along as my sidekick (my son Matthew was still too young). We completed 33 acts that day. Some activities were planned, many unplanned. I remember going into a Dollar Store where I handed Claire five single dollar bills, instructing her to place them in and around the toy aisle so that another child might find them and be able to buy something unexpected. She carefully selected the Rapunzel jigsaw puzzle and the jewel-encrusted tiara. The light in her eyes was so bright it could have taken out the sun. We picked up trash at a local park and handed out candy canes to strangers at the grocery store. So many great memories of that day.

The memory that holds the most space in my heart was from the hospital. We entered the facility with a dozen roses and stopped at the front desk to inquire as to a floor of patients that may need some cheer, but well enough to take visitors. We were sent to the third-floor rehab, patients recovering from hip replacements and knee surgeries. We stepped off the elevator. I approached the charge nurse and told her of our mission. She was moved by the idea and gestured down the hallway where we could begin. Claire went in and out of each room, handing patients a single rose and wishing them a speedy recovery. The response was overwhelming. Some patients were shy and confused, others spent long stretches of time telling us all about their grandchildren.

But the heart-stopping moment came as we were leaving.

Unbeknownst to me, the charge nurse had spread the word about our mission to the other staff on that floor. As we rounded the corner, there was a group of nurses standing in line to hug my daughter. To commend her determination for putting generosity and warmth into the world. Witnessing people stand in line to honor my child's heart was one of the greatest pleasures of my life. It was indescribable.

The day exceeded my expectations, with countless encounters of laughter, love, and learning. We definitely achieved our goal; we saw the light. And it grew brighter every day that followed. The tradition has continued each year since, adding more acts and spreading more kindness. The stories are countless, and the impact is endless. The Birthday Mission changed the way I look at the world, and more importantly, it has framed the way my children will for years to come. It continually reminds me of our innate ability to tap into the universe. Even in the darkest moments, one can find light in the world.

There is always light, if only we're brave enough to see it.
If only we're brave enough to be it.
—Amanda Gorman

Abundance challenge

As evidenced in the story above, we all have the ability to work with the abundance of the universe to create our desired outcomes. One simple and impactful way to leverage this theory in your own life is to take the abundance challenge. Begin the challenge by completing the sentence below:

I wish I had more _____ in my life.
Ex. Money, positivity, happiness, love, empathy.

Now, brainstorm ways in which you can generate more of your identified need for others.
Ex. Share job with others through text messages and social media posts.

Connecting the abundance of the universe to your purpose reinforces your conviction toward your desired change.

Be poised to step with courage

My sister once quipped that I had a way of making lemonade out of grapefruits. She was referencing my cat-like ability to always land on my feet, regardless of the height of the fall. Whether this comes naturally to me or not, I know the effort that goes into a life of lemonade-making. All that we have discussed so far is bringing you to the very edge of the precipice.

Consider: whether life hands you lemons, grapefruits, job loss, or a bad relationship, you have a choice. You set the tone with your mindset. When faced with a difficult situation, think first about what positives you can take away. Then find what serves you—the good parts (flavors, zest)—and be willing to throw out/ dismiss the rest (seeds, hard exterior). This will give you a courageous state of mind every time.

Our commitment to our purpose is displayed most prominently in times of chaos, when the stakes are high, and the future is unknown. An available opportunity is not enough. You must be ready to seize the opportunity. This requires a mindset poised to step courageously. It requires an understanding that our natural inclination towards safety and the status quo is just that—an inclination. The resistance you feel is perfectly normal and part of your biological response, not an indicator that you should stop taking bold action in pursuit of dreams.

Courage in Action

Letting Go

You've identified the change you wish you make in Part One, you've explored your values and purpose in Part Two, now consider what you need to let go of for this change to take place. What habits or behaviors are standing in your way?

Ex. Spending too much time on social media affects my self-esteem.

_____

_____

Where are some opportunities you haven't participated in or considered in the past that could contribute to your values and purpose?

Ex. I could find an online support group to feed my need for screen time and motivate me at the same time.

_____

_____

Your Growth Mindset

Choose one of the habits or behaviors above that stand in the way of your desired change. Use this as your trigger or activating event (discussed in Chapter 15) to establish your growth mindset around your desired change.

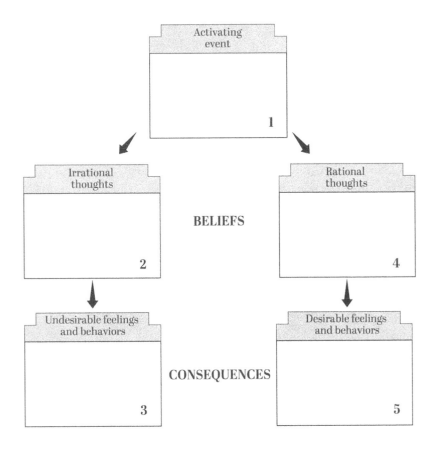

Anchor Question

One manner of attaching to our conviction is using anchor questions. Leveraging the same theory that makes powerful questions so prodigious, we develop an anchor question to act as a stronghold for our change. Let's walk through the steps below to create yours.

First, consider what prominent elements in your life might serve as a guidepost by which you make decisions. Write these below.

Ex. Promise to a loved one, what I hope people say about me in my eulogy, etc.

_____

_____

Then, review the statements above and craft an anchor question you can pose to yourself throughout this change that will continually ground you to your beliefs:

Ex. What will make me most proud when my transformation is complete?

_____

_____

Part 4:

Constancy

con·stan·cy | ˈkänstənsē

noun: the quality of being enduring; faithful and dependable

Chapter 17

Endurance

IIIIIIIIIIIIIIIIIIIIIIII

The clock was ticking. Claire was set to start kindergarten the following year. I had targeted the school district I wanted the kids to attend and, after doing so, moved us from one apartment to another to optimize my house search.

I viewed a For Sale by Owner home with my parents in the fall. The house looked great on the outside but had a choppy floor plan and wallpaper from floor to ceiling in every room. It didn't fit the image I had in my mind. I got a new real estate agent and kept looking. We must have looked at a million properties that winter. We went from house to house every weekend. I'd occasionally find something I like, make a bid, and, invariably, something would go wrong. I even offered above the asking price to one seller and they still turned me down.

The search continued. I so desperately wanted a yard for the kids to play in by summer. I was tired of watching for cars in the apartment parking lot. I was tired of coming home to a door that wasn't ours—like a daily reminder my plans had gone awry. Meanwhile, I was going to therapy to help juggle kids, hold down my corporate job, and maintain some semblance of a social life.

Finally, I broke.

Yet another seller backed out of a deal at the last minute. I cried, "Uncle." Told my agent I needed some time to step away, checked in with my doctor, and started a prescription for antidepressants. It was late March and time was running short. So was my patience.

Late one night, during my typical routine with Matthew (it took him a few years to learn to sleep after his colic), I rushed in to soothe his crying before he disturbed his sister sleeping just a few feet away. Too tired to do anything else, I brought him in to lay down with me. He tossed and turned in fits as he fell back asleep, ending with a sudden kick to the side of my head.

I opened my eyes to find tiny round toes inches from my face and thought, "I should hold onto this moment. One of these days I'm going to look back and miss his little feet." Sensing my change in perspective, I immediately recognized that my meds must be working. Funny, but true.

My mind started to wander to new optimism. I flashed back to the house that I had walked through in November. I recalled how it contained many of the structural elements I wanted, was in my target neighborhood, and had a great backyard. Cosmetically not right, but—there in the late hours of the night—I finally saw its potential.

The next morning, I called my real estate agent. Thirty-six hours later, I signed the paperwork to buy that house. And it is where I sit today. I look around at these beautiful walls (no longer covered in wallpaper). These walls echo the sounds of laughter when my kids are playing with friends. They contain all the latest smart home technology that my husband Rick prides himself on installing. These walls lead to a front door that reminds me of strength and courage every time I walk through. A door that is ours.

Kris McGuigan
April 20, 2013 ·

In ten days, I will open my front door. In a little over a week, I will have cell phone reception. I can park outside of my garage without receiving a ticket. I can get a glass of water after 10pm without fearing it will wake a sleeping toddler. In ten days, my kids will have a yard in which to play. Matthew can sing himself to sleep for hours in his own bedroom without interrupting his sister's beauty rest. Claire can have her own drawing table, a block to ride her bike around, and space for her dollhouse to be open all the time. The only feet I will hear scampering above me will be those of my children. In ten days, I will reach a milestone on this path I set out on exactly two years ago. I will show my daughter (and son) how to be your own hero.
In ten days, I will be home.

🖤👍 60   12 Comments 2 Shares

This post from my Facebook page embodies the power and pride I was feeling during this time. It is alarming but satisfying to juxtapose the sentiments above with the sadness and hopelessness I shared online during the months prior. The home purchase was a major turning point in my life. Reaching this milestone proved to me once and for all that I could do anything I set my mind to.

Constancy is the *how* of courage. It is about action. Enduring. Doing. Establishing daily practices that breed resolve and build resilience. The quality of endurance is that of getting up, again and again, no matter how many times you fall. The work of clarity illuminated who you are and what you want. Conviction has readied your mind and environment for success. It is time to step through the fear and into action. It is time for constancy.

My home search-and-find was an act of endurance. When we commit to this approach, we give ourselves permission to take any step—even small and seemingly insignificant strides—in the right direction. Reevaluating the plan at frequent intervals. Burning the plan when needed. Being open to new plans.

The Four Pillars of Constancy

Over the years of guiding myself and my clients through countless changes, I have observed several trends in one's approach, action, posture, and environment that contribute to successful transitions. I formulated these themes into an easy-to-follow framework, allowing you to apply constancy to any change you undertake.

The Four Pillars of Constancy
1. **Doing** above **Thinking**
2. **Manageable** above **Monumental**
3. **Pausing** above **Pushing**
4. **Support** above **Setbacks**

We will explore each of the four pillars in the chapters ahead. As you look to apply these concepts, keep in mind that constancy is to be continuous, repeatable, and fluid. Real. Raw. Final but unfinished. Unlike consistency that demands a robotic representation of sameness regardless of life circumstance, constancy allows for authenticity. Constancy is where consistency meets resilience. It is where we forgive ourselves for missteps and gain the strength and courage to keep going.

Chapter 18

Doing above Thinking

||||||||||||||||||||||

The first pillar of constancy speaks to the approach you take to change. It is predicated on the fact that we learn and progress exponentially more from doing than thinking.

Take a moment to contemplate the last project or program you worked on (ex. collaboration with the executive team; setting a schedule; presentation delivered; etc.). Reflect on both the time you spent planning the work as well as the time you spent executing or doing the work. Now step back and reflect. I want you to consider: Where did most of the learning take place? In which facet of the project were you able to really dig in and understand more about how to get it done and produce the desired result?

We learn more through the application of our thoughts as opposed to the formulation. As New York Times bestselling author Grant Cardone points out, "most people desire success and have great ideas but they come up short on the amount of action required to get their lives to the exceptional levels they deserve."[42]

Brainstorming is a phenomenal practice, but nothing offers more quick and relevant data than the practice of doing.

Most people think they should have all their ducks in a row before proceeding with any major, or even minor, plan. Instead, consider the smallest action you can take to begin to explore a means to achieve your desired direction. Then take quick and deliberate action to test that path. Try to find joy in even the difficult parts and strive to improve yourself each and every day.

Remain adaptable. When the action leads to positive results, continue. When the action causes a misstep, re-assess and consider a new action. With each iteration, demonstrate control, not over the outcome but over your response to it.

When I first quit my job to start my business, my mother gifted me a decorative sign that read:

IF YOU'RE WAITING FOR THE RIGHT TIME, IT'S NOW.

She wasn't telling me my timing was perfect. Quite the opposite. She was saying no time would be perfect. We must step courageously into the future with what we have available, improving and adapting *while in motion*. Doing above thinking is the linchpin to stepping through the fear and into courageous change.

Progress over perfection

Think of something you care for: if you are a parent, your children certainly fit the mark. Pet and plant parents, you're here too. Maybe you are a loving and compassionate friend who offers unending support and a shoulder to cry on.

Now, tell me: did you know how to provide the right care from day one? Do you always know exactly the right thing to do or say?

Of course not. You feel it out as you go. Bring a consistent approach while altering your style as needed. Stick with it even as it gets hard. As caregivers and companions, we take progress over perfection because there is no alternative.

We are inundated with messages about the wrong way to do things as compared to the way we're doing them (also known as the wrong way). This happens in our personal and professional space. We strive to find the right career, produce the desired results, all while balancing work and life without even a drop of sweat on our foreheads. We expect perfection right out of the gate. We glamorize overworking and extreme achievement from a very early age. We are convinced there is a perfect path, and most of the time, we're not on it.

RESEARCH SPOTLIGHT

According to the Pew Research Center, seventy-two percent of people in the United States now use social media with 2.89 billion users on Facebook alone.[43] At its core, social media is a powerful communication tool that has fundamentally changed how individuals interact with one another. Online communities have sped up the exchange of information and ideas but have also taken their toll on our mental health.

With the prevalence of curated content, social networks can lead to the altered and inaccurate impression of the physical and personality traits of other users. This can result in incorrect conclusions regarding physical appearance, educational level, intelligence, moral integrity, as well as many other characteristics of online friends.

In return, users themselves may demonstrate a "hyper-personal model" of behavior during computer-mediated communication when using an online platform, because the subject has more time to select, emphasize, and present those aspects of their personality, character, and temperament that would be viewed more favorably by the receivers or, in this case, other Facebook users.

Constant self-evaluation on an everyday basis, competition and comparing one's own achievements with those of other users, incorrectly perceiving physical/emotional/social characteristics of others, feeling of jealousy, and narcissistic behavior—these are all factors that may positively or negatively influence self-esteem.[44]

Our online voice offers a window into the type of persona we are through what we post, who we tag, and which location is referenced. The kinds of people we allow ourselves to be are influenced not only by our voices, but by the voices of others and their interests too. Yet, the way we interact and react when we get fewer likes than expected tells us more about our real identities than a single photo or video ever could.

Perpetual beta

Meanwhile, we invest thousands of dollars each year and hours every day relying on a tool that from which we expect—accept and are even excited by—imperfection. It's likely within your reach right now: your smartphone.

When upgrades are pushed to my iPhone, I usually want to tear my hair out. My home screen has different commands and various buttons are not where I remembered them. Yet, while I'm struggling to learn the nuances of the latest improvements, at no time do I blame Apple's CEO. I trust Tim Cook and his team are making it better for me. This is a result of tech companies—apps, gaming, phones—establishing an ongoing culture of perpetual beta.

Perpetual beta is defined as keeping a software or a system at the beta development stage for an extended or indefinite period of time. Perpetual: continuous; everlasting; ongoing. Beta: a *nearly complete* prototype of a product. Often used to release new features that may not be fully tested, this iterative methodology lends itself to a much more rapid and nimble approach to development, staging, and deployment. The developers and marketers and all the brilliance that exists within a monster corporation such as Apple bring forth the best they can and then simply let it go. They allow the market reaction and real-time testing to do the rest. They somehow make you and me, as customers, perfectly happy with an imperfect product.

Like a banana picked before it is ready, the product is placed in the hands of the consumer to let it ripen. The benefits of doing so are clear. It provides faster access to the latest features, allows for easy course correction, enables quick recovery from failure, removes the pressure to get it right, and highlights the boldest, most effective learning tool we have: feedback.

Essential in the tech world, perpetual beta can be applied to the human experience, granting once and for all permission for imperfection. It can apply to going live with a beta website, installing a new app to manage the family calendar, or trying a new dinner routine. You can employ the same principles and bask in the glory of experimentation following the simple steps below:

When considering the first aspect of change to be made, **aim for a low-risk environment** that will require minimal time, energy, or emotional pull. Keep in mind that strong information stems from simple tests, and that doing trumps thinking: don't overthink it.

Test your idea as quickly as possible. Give it a try.

When finished, **review the outcome**. Did it work? What did you learn? How can you apply the energy for your first test to generate the next one? The review does not need an in-depth analysis with a scientist by your side. As best-selling author Mel Robbins states, "Your inner wisdom is a genius. Your goal-related impulses, urges, and instincts are there to guide you. Learn to bet on them."[45] **Continue to test** and learn as many times as needed to pick up steam and make progress toward your desired goal. Embrace the change and have fun along the way.

Contemplating a career change by quitting your job to work at the circus is an expensive (monetarily and emotionally) proposition. But what if you took a side job on the weekends picking up peanuts to learn more about the environment and begin to cultivate relationships from the inside out? Less extreme, and easier to navigate when you realize it was the animals you loved all along and perhaps a position as a vet tech may be a better fit than a ringmaster.

You have been taught by decades of motivational giants to think in extremes (ex. live your dream life, make a move from poverty to extreme wealth). These far-reaching goals can be exciting. You are prompted to build strategies and complex plans to get there. But this approach does not allow for easy course correction that will invariably be needed when you experience disruption when life—or your plan—doesn't work out as expected. Think instead of enjoying the process and improving yourself (and your life) along the way. Heed advice from a youth flag football coach I overheard in the huddle just before a heated game of nine-year-old shenanigans:

Have fun. Get better.

Visit therequisitecourage.com/bonusmaterials to download a guide to experimenting with small changes to make big impact in your life.

Expect turbulence

I travel often for work and pleasure, locally and internationally. It's rare to be on even a short flight wherein you don't experience turbulence. It is a common occurrence; the flight crew calmly addresses the bumps in the air by notifying the passengers and requesting we all stay seated until the disturbance has passed. You see, turbulence is expected. It is not a cause for panic. It does not dictate the plane be turned around and headed back to its origin. It is to be tolerated as a normal part of the luxury of reaching new heights.

Life rarely goes as planned. Stephen Hawking was diagnosed with ALS at the age of twenty-one and given two more years to live, before going on to become an eminent scientist and one of the most recognizable celebrities of our time.[46] Soichiro Honda, the late founder of the Honda Motor Company, was forced to pawn his wife's wedding ring just to stay afloat after his first two businesses failed.[47] Bethany Hamilton was a competitive surfer at age thirteen when a shark attack severed her left arm. She successfully returned to the world of professional surfing, adding numerous sports awards and acting credits to her portfolio.[48] These and so many other determined individuals exemplify the power of looking beyond challenges and ahead to opportunities.

As you focus on doing above thinking, expect turbulence. Recall our learnings about the fear of the unknown. Traverse the uncertainty by finding strength in clarity. Allot time to contemplate your core principles while setting a goal. Identify which values you will adhere to along the route. These values will serve as guideposts, allowing for the flexibility to alter your path as needed while still keeping your eye on the goal.

Focus on what you can control. In his book *The 7 Habits of Highly Effective People*, Stephen R. Covey distinguished between proactive people who focus on what they can do and influence and reactive people who focus energy beyond their control. "It was only…when we focused on our own paradigms that we began to create positive energy that changed ourselves."[49]

EVENT + RESPONSE = OUTCOME

The most successful people in life love being uncomfortable. Resilient people embody an uncanny ability to improvise. Embed missteps into your plan and grant yourself permission to fall down along the way.

More than education, more than experience, more than training, a person's level of resilience will determine who succeeds and who fails. That's true in the cancer ward, it's true in the Olympics, and it's true in the boardroom.
—Dean Becker

Visit therequisitecourage.com/bonusmaterials to download a guide to making bold decisions that are actionable.

Chapter 19

Manageable above Monumental

||||||||||||||||||||||

The second pillar of constancy relates to the actions we take. More specifically, the size of the actions we take. If we are being expected to endure, small and digestible steps are the key to success.

William S. Harley and Arthur Davidson first developed the idea of a motorized bike when meeting up at their favorite fishing hole. They envisioned creating a faster mode of transportation that would require less effort and generate more fun.

The men recruited Arthur's brother Walter and got to work on their first prototype. Avoiding a large investment in equipment and facilities, they set up shop in a shed in the backyard. The first model was finished in 1903. While the test was mostly successful, the bike was unable to climb hills without the rider providing pedaling assistance.

But Harley and the Davidson brothers did not give up. They immediately began working on a new and improved machine. They created a bigger engine and loop-frame design. After completing the prototype in 1904, they entered the bike into a local motorcycle race at the State Fair Park, where it placed fourth.

Now that they had a working model, bare Harley-Davidson engines were listed in the January 1905 Automobile and Cycle Trade Journal. Just four months later, the motorcycles were in production. That first year, five bikes were produced. The second year in the factory, fifty bikes were produced. And one hundred fifty the year after that. Harley-Davidson is now one of the world's largest motorcycle manufacturers with an iconic brand and a loyal following. All because the founders took small steps—baby steps—toward a big vision.[50]

Why step like a baby? One might discern because they are smaller steps on those tiny legs and seem less scary. Well, I've got news for you—it's not the distance that eliminates fear for the child. Proportionally, the size of that four-inch movement can be pretty terrifying. And the resulting bump on your rump when you hit the ground? Also frightening. Yet babies don't stop. They keep getting back up. Again, and again. Because the fear of not making it across the room to grab that doggie's tail is greater than the fear of falling. Toddlers are smart enough (in many cases, smarter than adults) to know that falling doesn't equal failure, it just means they are getting some good reps in.

Fear can be crippling. And the bottom line is that fear is unavoidable. The desire to elude pain is in our genetic makeup. Yet, research has shown again and again that the only way to eliminate it is to do the thing that scares you. Conversely, the extraordinary thing about facing your fear is that it gives you power. Instantly. The moment you take on the fear, you are reminded you are a strong and capable being. You are better prepared for the next. By facing your fear, you take away the power it has over you and transfer that power and strength to yourself. You can also build courage like a muscle. You exercise it daily, and each time it is strengthened. Just ask the nearest toddler, afraid to take a step or climb a jungle gym for the first time.

You can flex courage like a muscle the same way you can build strength at the gym. Baby steps enhance trust in yourself. Just as William and Arthur started small with what they had, doing something now will always bring you closer to your goal than not. Every action brings more momentum. Every time you act on your decisions, keeping your promise to yourself by honoring your intention, you build self-esteem.

How small steps lead to big change

Malcolm Gladwell popularized the concept of the ten-thousand-hour rule in his bestselling book *Outliers*. Gladwell describes the rule as such: it takes ten thousand hours of intensive practice to achieve mastery of complex skills and materials, like mastering chess or getting as good at playing the cello as Yo-Yo Ma.[51] There have been arguments since Gladwell's theory was popularized that all practice is not equal. But whether or not you believe ten thousand is the exact number, we all see the theory in practice every day watching professional sports. Basketball legend Michael Jordan is noted as practicing up to eight hours a day. He often advised, "Get the fundamentals down and the level of everything you do will rise."

AUTHOR SPOTLIGHT

Truth be told, I was terrified of the sound of my own voice when I first embarked on my public speaking career. My speech practice included reading the script over and over, endless times in my head. That's right. I wasn't even saying it out loud. I quickly found this method, while less scary, was not effective. I began recording presentations using a voice app on my phone and then listening back. While this form of review helped with the memorization of content, it still had little effect on my performance.

My next attempt at rehearsals included a full video recording on my computer, watched back for cues and refinement. The nuances of my tone and speed as well as areas requiring more transitional content came through. Still, I seemed to be missing the mark. It was time for intentional practice. I needed a real audience.

I joined a local Toastmasters International group and began delivering speech content in a real-life setting with real-life spectators. The human element exceeded any simulation I was able to create at home. Moreover, it allowed for the receipt of critical feedback on my delivery and content. I was able to refine my approach until my words were fully resonating with others. I was finally learning to master my craft.

Years later, the principle holds. I have found time and again that no matter how great of a speech I write, it requires multiple attempts at delivery before it truly hits an audience.

The positive results that stem from constant behavior are initially imperceptible by the doer. Like a colicky baby that begins to wean from an extended cry, yet the mother is too tired and traumatized to notice. Like the manager conducting weekly one-on-one meetings supplemented by on-the-spot team training who fails to notice the performance report demonstrating an upward turn. The outcomes of the tiny habit seeds you plant peek through the soil ever-so-slightly. It may take a budding flower to notice the results of your careful cultivation of effort and execution.

Crossing the finish line

To demonstrate breaking things out step-by-step, let's take a page from marathon runners.

The internet is chock full of advice and training plans to support novice runners to make it to the finish line. These plans do not start with "Run ten miles." That would be crazy and a surefire way to keep people on their couch as opposed to the track.

The recommended training process typically begins with a self-assessment around your current activity level, the timeline in which you hope to race, etc. From there, you are directed to a suggested routine that builds from week to week. Day one, for example, may be a short walk.

But what if you're still overwhelmed by the idea of walking a mile tomorrow morning? No need to give up your goal of running the race, simply break it down even more.

Day 1. Set alarm.
Day 2. Wake up to alarm.
Day 3. Wake up and think about running for two minutes before hitting the snooze button.
Day 4. Wake up and get out of bed and think about running.
Day 5. Wake up and get out of bed and put your running shoes on.
Day 6. Wake up, get out of bed, put your running shoes on and stand outside for 3 minutes.

You get the idea. The human brain continually reorganizes itself by forming new neural connections throughout life. This

phenomenon is known as neuroplasticity. We can build strong
pathways to our desired goals through small, repetitive activity.
You don't need to run a full marathon. You need only do the next
brave thing: Wake up and think about running. Make it so easy
that you can't say no.

Think of your identified change. What is one step you can
take to put the change into action:

1. _____
_____

Now break that step down into 5 smaller steps.

a. _____
_____

b. _____
_____

c. _____
_____

d. _____
_____

e. _____
_____

Review step one. Can that be broken down even smaller? Now
assign a start date.

i. _____
starting _____
ii. _____
starting _____
iii. _____
starting _____

Positioning for the first step

As you prepare to tackle these fears and step into courageous living, you may be feeling a bit of trepidation, hesitation, or all-out panic. That's a natural part of the process.

To bring your feelings into alignment for all you are about to encounter, take a moment and tap into your posture power. Former FBI agent and body language expert Joe Navarro has written numerous books on projecting confidence through body language. Navarro observes various celebrities and politicians and demonstrates the things that they do that help them appear confident to others.[52] But strong poses can help you appear confident on the inside as well.

One of Harvard professor Amy Cuddy's most celebrated techniques is that of a *Power Position*. The basic idea is that you devise a physical movement that you repeatedly practice when you're in a positive mental state. This same procedure is used in training dogs to pull weighted sleds over long distances—starting with a small load and lots of encouragement until towing becomes associated with favorable emotions. Over time, your movement will become associated with feeling happy and focused. You will be able to trigger these emotions and enter your "peak state" by performing this movement.[53]

Start by thinking of a time in the past when you faced your fear. You confronted something you had trepidation about, allowed the fear to wash over you, and then did it anyway. Now, recall a time you felt powerful. Happy. Successful. Remember how your body was positioned at that time: Were you standing tall, with your chin up and your shoulders back? Were your feet planted firmly on the ground? Did you reverberate your arms? Fists up and lip curled in domination?

Jot down some of the positions that came to mind along with
the emotions they brought forth in the table below.

Body Position	Emotions Elicited
Ex. Stand up, arms in a body-builder pose.	**Ex.** Confidence, energy, ready to conquer anything.

Now pick one and get up and try. Right now. Stand up and
bust a move. Commit to trying one or more of these power moves
over the next 48 hours when you feel hesitant to take bold action.

**Visit therequisitecourage.com/bonusmaterials to download a
guide to making bold decisions that are manageable.**

Chapter 20

Fear of Isolation

||||||||||||||||||||

Before we get to the third pillar of constancy, let's pause to discuss something many of us encounter, consciously and unconsciously. Moving fearlessly through courage and simultaneously shifting away from your perfectly curated persona can be isolating. You may no longer be the person you were to others, the leader you were to your team, or the shoulder everyone else came to cry on. The fear of being unrecognized or left behind can trigger an unwanted and inauthentic response. Standing alone in your conviction can feel isolating at first. To combat loneliness, we often return to presenting as staged versions of ourselves in hopes of making people like us.

Think of the last time you went on a date: was there a moment(s) you exaggerated the truth in hopes of being accepted? The last time you updated your resume, did you feel a ping to overplay past success in hopes of being more marketable?

Rather than offer a false sense of self, offer instead a false level of self-assurance. There is immense power and influence in manifesting the confidence you desire by acting as though it is already within you. From a very early point in my career, I acted like there was a place at the table for me even when there wasn't. When I was an administrative assistant brought to the board meeting to take notes, instead of sitting in the back of the room, I just sat at the table. When I joined the Rotary Club as the youngest-ever member, I dismissed the "What is she doing here?" chatter and found a place at the table. In fact, at distinct times in my career, I sat down *before* there was a space at the table.

They say that you should dress for the role that you want next. I think that you should behave in the role that you want next. I'm not suggesting you take authority or position that has not been given to you. Yet, there is something to be said for making sure the world knows that you are ready. Demonstrate that you're willing to work for it. Volunteer for new assignments. Showcase your skills with a special project. Attend association meetings before joining the industry. The more you believe in your placement, the more it believes in you.

Ask for what you want

In addition to acting the part, verbalizing your interests can portray a high sense of confidence as well. Owning your space, your strength, and your value means being willing to raise your hand and speak up.

In my work, I often encounter clients who are hoping for something more, but taking little action to make it happen:

- A speaker suffering from impostor syndrome was struggling to raise his fees.
- An employee hesitant to ask for the promotion.
- An adult daughter seeking respect from her overbearing mother.

Together, we talk through options, wants, and needs. We reflect on their values to recall why this ask is an important, values-based appeal. Then, I encourage them to make the ask. The real ask. State what they actually want, not what they think they will get. When they tell me with feigned certainty that they will be told no, I point out that if you're going to get turned down either way, you might as well ask for the good stuff.

CLIENT SPOTLIGHT

Years ago, a coworker and friend confided in me about an interview she had in another department at the hospital and the expectation of a pending job offer. Sarah presented the news with a mix of excitement and panic. She had never negotiated a salary before and the anticipation of the call from HR was inducing anxiety.

Fresh on the heels of starting my business, I offered some low-risk coaching: I can help boost your confidence and refine your negotiation approach in exchange for a small percentage of the increase you receive.

I walked Sarah through the justification process, including how to complete market research on current pay rates for similar positions and how to prepare accomplishment statements showcasing how her prior work had positively impacted the company's bottom line.

After setting high, medium, and low targets, Sarah acclimated to her new goal by repeating an affirmation multiple times each day. We worked together to build her confidence and eliminate mental roadblocks and self-limiting beliefs (remember that pesky fear of inadequacy from Chapter 13?). When the call finally came, she made the ask.

When negotiations were over, Sarah had secured a twelve percent increase in salary. And I had secured my first official client success story.

Stop underselling yourself. Next time, declare that you are worth it. Admit that you have put in the work. Admit that you are uniquely qualified for this opportunity. Admit to your awesomeness. Admit it again and again. The more we admit we have value, the more that valuable opportunities present themselves.

Chapter 21

Pausing above Pushing

|||||||||||||||||||||||||||||

The third pillar of constancy speaks to one's frame of mind. Specially, the framing that lends itself to an unceasing drive for success without reprieve. Life is full of ups and downs. Systems preaching "consistency at all costs" sets people up to think they need to be superhuman. And that's not realistic.

In our quest for courage, there are days we won't show up. There are days that we won't want to get out of bed. There are days that we drop the plates that we are supposed to be spinning. It doesn't matter how good you've become at self-discovery or unwavering conviction; you will always be a human being.

CLIENT SPOTLIGHT

I encountered a jobseeker named John who was exhausted and overwhelmed. For months, he had been working his regular nine-to-five job and would come home and work late into the night, pouring loads of time and energy into his search. I could hear the fatigue in his voice. He was nervous about an upcoming family vacation that had been on the calendar for over a year. Worried he couldn't cancel the trip without disappointing his family but couldn't take a break from his search without the floor dropping out from underneath him. After some reframing and assurance, the time away might be best, John headed to the Caribbean. Upon his return, with renewed energy and spark, John nailed an interview with his first-choice employer. Turns out the rest and rejuvenation did him good.

For years, in life and business, I thought consistency was the key to success. Be reliable. Unphased. Always present. I applied this regimen to my brand, to my parenting, and even to my physical appearance.

Don't let them see you sweat.

Don't flinch; don't fall.

Don't fail.

But eventually, the realities of running a multi-faceted business and a family left me humbled. My commitment to steadiness did not leave any room for healing when facing inevitable flinching and failing.

Angela Duckworth is the best-selling author and world's leading authority on grit. Beginning her own education at Harvard University, she faced opposition and difficulty passing a neurobiology class. Her professor recommended dropping the course, but Duckworth responded with obstinance and instead selected neurobiology as her major. She recalls being a very determined student, but definitely not always happy and relaxed.

Duckworth then landed a demanding job at a management consulting firm after college. Still, the sense of satisfaction and tranquility evaded her. She eventually felt called to help others navigate the troubled waters she herself experienced and left her job to teach math to seventh graders in New York City Public Schools. It was here she observed the high correlation between effort and success, determining grit is obtainable without unrelenting exertion.[54]

You see, rigid consistency does not allow for restorative resilience. What if I know that I'm supposed to be consistent and produce a podcast once a week, or always be available to my clients, but I need to care for an elderly parent? What if I have a splitting migraine? True resilience is predicated upon a willingness to take pause, practice tireless and unapologetic self-care, self-forgiveness, and rest.

And on a deeper level, rigid consistency does not leave a lot of space for authenticity, either. When I am pushing myself beyond my limits, I am responding to fear (of inadequacy, isolation, etc.) as opposed to living from a place of courage. The constant churn of needing to always be "on" is far from being my true and best self.

Our greatest glory is not in never falling,
but in rising every time we fall.
—Confucius

Living courageously requires personal grace. You must exercise kindness and clemency toward yourself when things go wrong. When you fall off the wagon, you must give yourself the chance to get back on. Grant yourself reprieve from self-inflicted guilt and punishment for missing the mark. Rather than see the misstep as a setback, see it as a sign from the universe that it is time for a pause. You might consider:

- Combatting your inner critic by reciting your favorite positive affirmations aloud.
- Taking a walk in the middle of a stressful day.
- Moving deadlines and reevaluating priorities at regular intervals.
- Allowing yourself to try again if you got it wrong the first time.

Take a moment to pause (see what I did there?) and write down some ideas as to how you can implement more pauses into your daily life.

Ex. Set a "take a break" timer on my phone. Invite a colleague to walk every morning. Journal before bed each night.

_____

_____

_____

Consider also what triggers (feelings, behaviors, thoughts) may indicate a pause is needed. How will you know when you need to recharge?

Ex. Restless, overwhelmed. Start to jump at my kids when they ask for things. Spending too much time scrolling through my phone.

_____

_____

_____

Have you ever been in the presence of someone who extends themselves and others authentic forgiveness and second chances? Who takes the time to acknowledge shortcomings and then readily offers an extension of grace? Creating this sense of safety to pause and start again is as valuable to us as it is to others.

Recognize the journey

One tactic for finding pride along your journey to improvement is to illustrate to your mind just how far you have come. This can take the form of a list of achievements but can also be a single line drawn on the page.

The endpoint on the left represents a point in time of your past. You can choose your birth, the first day of school, the start of a new career, your first sale. Any earlier stage wherein you can identify a milestone associated with your current direction in life. The endpoint on the right is intended to represent your desired end point. This end may be the final deliverable on a project or an ideal state you aspire to reach.

Take an honest look at the timeline you've drawn and place an "X" on the line to represent where you feel you are along the spectrum.

where you started   where you're going

The left-hand side of the line offers a visual representation—one hard to dispute—of how far you truly have come. This quick but impactful exercise helps to ready your mind for the next challenge.

Joy on demand

There is a jar full of joy on my desk. Years ago, when I still worked in corporate America, I led a team-building exercise with my staff. We came together at a makeshift craft table with our mason jars and ribbon, and we created a simple, yet powerful means to produce joy on demand. The concept is somewhat of a grownup version of small children catching fireflies on a warm summer night. Remember how proud we were when we got one? Naively believing it would continue to glow for nights to come, failing to understand the lack of oxygen inside that tightly sealed jar.

The joy captured inside of *this* jar rarely needs air to breathe and can be cared for with only a passing glance. It is a treasure trove of sorts. I encouraged each team member to grab written documentation: a printed email, a copy of an award, a post-it with a memorable quote. This practice of compiling, over time, things that make you smile and feel proud will increase resiliency. Include written trinkets that remind you of the value you bring each and every day. Fill your jar to the brim. And when the days are long or the project seems endless, open up that jar. Release the paper within and soak in all those positive words. Affirmations. Reminders.

It need not be a mason jar and it doesn't have to be in plain sight. In whatever way you are comfortable, be sure to stockpile some joy. Establish a go-to method to call forward words of wisdom and inspiration during your moments of pause. Your future self will thank you for it.

Celebrate small wins

Milestones serve as good checkpoints for large projects and give us clues about our progress. They're important but they don't always occur frequently enough to serve their purpose. Often, these markers of success fall short of keeping us on the right path when the going gets tough.

Measuring your own success doesn't have to model anyone else's track record. Rather than wait for a full mile to pass, what about recognizing each yard that passes? Each foot? Take an intentional pause to celebrate success in small wins along the way. Over time, you will gather momentum for the journey. Remind yourself that you've made more progress toward your goal than you think.

Consider the last time you implemented a health goal in your life. Most people would tell you to celebrate the final pound lost or the twenty-sixth mile run. But what if you instead set an intention to celebrate the first day you woke up with more energy or the first three-day running streak?

Capture some of your favorite ways to celebrate below. Consider activities and/or small rewards that may feed your soul after a job well done.

Ex. Dinner and a movie, buy a new book, take the afternoon off.

_____

_____

_____

Visit therequisitecourage.com/bonusmaterials to download a guide to making bold decisions that breed resilience.

Chapter 22

Support above Setbacks

||||||||||||||||||||||

The final pillar of constancy is that of creating an environment that provides support in the face of inevitable setbacks. We've focused so far on much of the inner work that goes into courage. But the factors and people upon which we rely can contribute or distract from our ability to execute courageous change.

Several months after leaving my corporate job to start a career management firm, I was feeling lost and stagnant. I knew I had the expertise but was unsure as to how to translate that knowledge into a sustainable business. I had done hours—days even—of research and given myself all the pep talks one could give. I began to recognize a need for external support. I needed a confidante. Someone to share ideas with. Someone to listen. To help me stay on track and stay sane.

Fortunately, the simple acknowledgment of my need was enough to trigger the universe to present none other than business coach extraordinaire, Kim. I hired Kim almost immediately after an introductory consult and, years later, still call upon her guidance and support monthly.

Change can be frightening, disruptive, and isolating. How can you be intentional about creating an environment that will position you for success in the face of setbacks? Let's explore some ways you can combat the detrimental nature of upsets and learn to lean into the right kind of support.

Environmental factors

Situating your situation is going to be really important when you begin the work of courage. As we've said before, there is only so much you can control around you. Read through the categories below and identify areas where you can create an environment more conducive to change.

Physical and Mental Health. Take inventory of your basic needs and be honest with yourself as to whether they are being met. Are you getting enough water, nutrients, and sleep? Assess your mental health. Does your level of stability and balance support success? If not, what needs to change?

Risk/Security. To ensure your risk tolerance is in line with actions being taken, consider your current level of financial support. Where might there be gaps? If making a significant change does not provide the needed level of security, consider a phased approach. Maintain open communication with those affected by the risks you take to ensure collaboration.

Physical Surroundings. Our immediate habitat plays a big role in both our attitude and posture towards work. Reflect on whether your physical space is prompting you to move in a positive direction or distracting from the task at hand. What needs to be present in your environment to help you thrive? Work to ensure your external space feeds your internal vibes.

Once you've identified areas of opportunities, develop an easy-to-follow plan to bring your environment more into alignment.

Interpersonal support

Even more than environmental factors, research suggests the strongest predictor of human resilience is interpersonal support.[55] Corporations rely on a board of directors to look out for the stakeholders' best interests. Board members bring skills and expertise, provide strategic direction, and establish frameworks for setting and reaching expectations. Once you know your strengths, talents, and values, you're ready to assemble your own team of resources to help keep you in alignment and advance your vision—a personal board of directors.[56]

Members of your personal board may be colleagues, community contacts, members of the professional sector, or other individuals you know and respect. Whether in a pre-established framework or gathering a support system as opportunities present themselves at work, a defined cohort of collaborators can offer a platform for knowledge sharing and a safe space for vulnerability about challenges and struggles.

In the workplace

The benefit of a group of people offering you advice and support as opposed to a single mentor is the value of combined expertise. Gathering perspectives from a variety of professionals with different skill sets and backgrounds will not only increase the frequency of support but the bandwidth as well. Mastermind groups are made up of powerhouse professionals and are often brought together under the umbrella of a formal, paid membership. Other masterminds are formed by a shared experience, industry, field, or set of goals.

At home

You are often called to courage in your personal life, so it is best to build an entourage there as well. A host of supporters who lift you up, cheer you on, and put you in your place. The personal branch of your board may include friends, family, barbers, babysitters, basketball spectators, etc. A thought partner that exudes empathy may be just the right balance to your extreme desire for justice. A coach that can shift your focus to action planning can help pull you out of the past.

AUTHOR SPOTLIGHT

My father worked tirelessly to provide for his family and always wanted what was best for his three children. As any good parent, he employed a delicate balance of guiding versus governing. It was my dad that coached me through my first-ever critical career conversation.

I was a senior in high school and, despite having very strong academic prospects and career aspirations that would require a bachelor's degree, I wanted to forego college. Embarrassing to admit, it was for a boy.

I can't speak for what I would do as a parent in that moment, but I doubt it would reflect the same calm and cool approach my father took to the conversation. The first cornerstone of coaching is a belief that the coachee is naturally creative, resourceful, and whole (commonly phrased: humans can come up with their own answers without being directed what to do). Holding to that notion, my dad held back his own bias and responded with curiosity. He inquired as to my longer-term plans and danced in the moment (the second cornerstone of coaching) by offering perspective and opportunities for self-awareness.

He never once told me what to do. He simply presented me with the facts, focusing the conversation in equal parts on my head, my heart, and my gut. This triad is the third cornerstone of coaching and prompted me to explore all options with a holistic view.

That day, my dad stood beside me as I contemplated a fork in the road. He allowed me to come to my own conclusion and feel safe in doing so. That conversation evoked lasting transformation—the final cornerstone—as I headed off to college that fall.

Be sure you have representatives from all areas of life, backgrounds, and perspectives. Someone who doesn't think or act like you do. Someone who will play the devil's advocate. Someone who speaks up for the underdog. Someone will look you right in the eye and tell you that you are doing it wrong. Someone who makes you laugh. Someone who supports you unconditionally. Therapists, coaches, accountants. For many, connecting with a spiritual figure provides comfort and stability.

Think of individuals you already have in your inner circle. People you can be authentic around and trust to provide critical feedback as needed. List their names/roles below.

Ex. Dad. Sister. neighbor. Cubicle mate. Personal trainer. Coach. Therapist.

_____

_____

_____

Reviewing the list, where might there be gaps in your entourage? Consider areas of your life that support a healthy mind, body, and soul. Then be sure to select individuals that meet the following criteria:

Trust. Honest feedback is a critical element to sustainable growth. We sometimes think we are better (or worse) than we really are. You may already rely on a colleague to give you feedback on your performance at work, or a friend who can offer you good tips on handling difficult conversations. Select trustworthy individuals whom you respect and whose opinion you value.

Expertise. Go outside your area of expertise to find individuals whose background and experiences complement your own. Think of people with the skills you want to improve or the experience you could learn from. Are you uncomfortable with something, such as new technology or public speaking? Think who might best answer your questions or be willing to help you learn. Think about whose career or work ethic you admire and who may be positioned to help you progress in a certain area of the company.

Perspective. Seek out individuals with different backgrounds, perspectives, and work experience or who are from different areas of the company or parts of the world that are new to you. We tend to hold on to our beliefs and assumptions in the absence of evidence to the contrary. You may be surprised at what you can learn by opening yourself to different input. An objective viewpoint can help us see our intention—our self-view—mirrored back to us.

Advocacy. Include an individual (or several) who has known you for a long time. Board members should be willing to champion you, build you up, and give you some time in the limelight. Immense ingenuity is sparked by the simple gesture of having someone believe in you. Existing relationships are also well suited to help you see your impact through the eyes of others.

List which roles you will seek out to bolster your support system in the next 1-3 months.

Ex. Career mentor. Financial advisor. Friend who I can turn to for comic relief. Accountability partner.

_____

_____

_____

The frequency with which you connect with each member of your board will depend on your individual needs. The important thing is to rely on these individuals for structured, committed feedback and support. You should be touching base with them at regularly established intervals: monthly, quarterly, annually. The objective is to assemble a group of diverse humans who have your back. They should be diverse in all directions: cultural background, thinking, skill set, and so on. They should bring a variety of experiences, fears, creative ideas, and aspirations.

Recognize also, just as directors have terms, different members of your personal board may ebb and flow over time. Consider how childhood friends translate into adulthood. Those you stay connected with and those you run into at a grocery store or a little league game after decades of not talking. Think of the coworkers you spent each morning with sharing stories at the water cooler but now only interact via social media around holidays and special occasions. You should take the time to assess at regular intervals. A change in job, life status, or achievement of a major milestone can all trigger a need to reassess and add or subtract members.

Visit therequisitecourage.com/bonusmaterials to download a guide to creating the right environment for making bold decisions.

Chapter 23

Fear of Success

||||||||||||||||||||||

The true mark of success, happiness, and fulfillment comes with authentic execution. Achieving what we set out to do is a means of genuine validation that is hard to replicate. Yet, as we get closer and closer to the summit, the resistance we feel grows. The risk of losing aspects of ourselves, the potential change to how we are perceived by others, and the likelihood of feeling lost in new territory heightens.

I had a powerful female reach out with a common problem not so commonly talked about. Karen found herself standing at a career crossroads: stay in a role that is comfortable and seemingly predictable or step into the unknown with a new position that promises a higher salary and more responsibility. Here's the kicker: her greatest struggle was the fear that this change may result in...success.

Marianne Williamson eloquently points out, "Our deepest fear is not that we are inadequate. Our deepest fear is that we are powerful beyond measure. It is our light, not our darkness that most frightens us."

Fearing our greatness robs the world of all that we have to offer. Hiding from our power, we limit ourselves so as to not upset others. Rather, it is these moments wherein we are watched by others, and we are called to set and reach new summits. Inspiring those who will follow. As stated in the introduction:

Stand in the dark or turn on the light. The choice is yours and the impact of your decision is exponential. When you turn on a light, others begin to see. The secret to authentic leadership is not in flawless strategy; it is in fearless execution. Turn on the light for yourself, find your courage and others will use your shine.

Go so far you can't go back

There is a Mayan archaeological site in northern Belize named Actun Tunichil Muknal. Visitors must hike a mile and a half before the cave entrance even comes into view. After gearing up, a tour guide leads you down a shallow stream into the unassuming opening wherein they provide a brief review of necessary safety procedures and reminders. The group continues inward, until the darkness engulfs you and the bulb on your helmet generates the only light. After ten minutes of spelunking, the guide pauses again to check in with the group: "This is the final stage wherein you can opt-out. If you feel this is too intense, you may wish to stay here until the group returns."

You mean stay here completely alone in this pitch-dark cave surrounded by bats and an inability to move for the next forty minutes until your friends return?! Um, no thank you. You see, by that point in the adventure, we had gone too far to stop. And life is like that sometimes. There is a strategy behind going too far to go back. The momentum starts to pull us forward into the fear almost unconsciously, and we are less likely to retreat into the status quo.

Clarity, conviction, and courage are gained along the journey. Whether doing so by distance, public accountability, or logistics, going too far to go back can be a strong motivator. Create an external source of accountability that will make it easier to keep going than to shy away. Make it as easy as possible to move forward, as difficult as you can to retreat.

Strategic opportunism

In nature, an opportunist organism is a species that can thrive in different environmental conditions. It takes advantage of whatever there is around it to survive. Therefore, in biology, the term is not derogatory rather an indicator of a species that is adaptable, flexible, and a successful survivor. Even the term survival of the fittest is all about opportunism. The creature that can exploit its environment most successfully is the one that survives. Organisms that cannot take advantage of opportunities flounder and eventually die.

Strategic opportunism brings us out of nature and into the business world. The term refers to "the ability to remain focused on long-term objectives while staying flexible enough to solve day-to-day problems and recognize new opportunities."[57] If you practice strategic opportunism, you respond to today's needs while not precluding tomorrow's visions. More importantly, you tackle the fear of success by preparing for success well in advance.

The challenge in today's ever-changing workplace is to maintain both flexibility and direction. Strategic opportunism can be an effective way to stay receptive to new information and opportunities—to eventualities not yet considered. Put yourself in a position that you're ready to seize any fortune that comes your way.

This could mean having your resume updated in preparation for the next internal promotion or call from a recruiter. It could take the form of extending kindness to everyone you encounter, never sure who may hold the key to your future. You may conduct an annual self-evaluation, assessing your values, purpose, and alignment, preparing for any courageous change you may face.

Be ready for the different opportunities and people that cross your paths. You never know when the catalyst to your next big change will appear.

Courage in Action

Let's review a few important things as you begin to move into the how of courage.

You've learned that clarity is the source of courage. Courage comes from knowing who you are. After identifying your strengths, weaknesses, and whys, you did the work to let go of that which does not serve you and pivot in the direction of your most authentic life. Your conviction fuels your purpose.

Take a few moments to review the work you did in the previous *Courage in Action* sections. It's time now to step courageously into all that you are, believe, and desire.

Clarity
Change you desire (page 82)
Ex. Exercise Consistently

_____

_____

Your purpose statement (page 86)
Ex. Fear of Unknown, Inadequacy

_____

_____

Conviction
Your anchor question (page 129)
Ex. I create goodness in the world by using the trauma I've experienced to help others.

_____

_____

_____

Now, let's apply the Four Pillars of Constancy to provide the framework you need for courageous living.

Remember, this is not about rigid perfection. It's about milestones with mitigation. Results with rest. Self-driven courage with self-loving kindness.

Experimenting With Change

To begin manifesting your desired change, focus on small tests you can try to move closer to your potential. The only courage that matters is the kind that gets you from one moment to the next.

What is *one* thing you could do to move in the direction of your desired change?

Ex. Start eating healthy.

_____

_____

_____

_____

Try to break down the above action item into even smaller tasks.

Ex. Make salads for lunch; drink smoothies for breakfast; limit food intake after 8pm.

_____

_____

_____

_____

What do you anticipate as roadblocks when pursuing this test?

Ex. Lack of time or money; getting too hungry to follow the plan.

_____

_____

Applying the Four Pillars of Constancy

Using the information you have outlined above, spend time below determining how you will employ the Four Pillars when stepping into your desired change.

How will you apply **Doing** above **Thinking** to your desired change?

Ex. Rather than plan out meals for the entire week, I will try to alter my diet for Monday and see how I feel.

_____

_____

How will you apply **Manageable** above **Monumental** to your desired change?

Ex. I will cut back on sweets after 8pm. After one week of success, I will eliminate all food intake after 8pm.

_____

_____

How will you apply **Pausing** above **Pushing** to your desired change?

Ex. Keep a list of my favorite recharge activities on my desk to reference whenever I start to feel overwhelmed.

_____

_____

How will you apply **Support** above **Setbacks** to your desired change?

Ex. Spend time rounding out my personal board of directors to include more people I can contact for encouragement.

_____

_____

When will you start? Using the actions you wrote from the Four Pillars, list them below with a date to start and a date for checking your progress.

Action	Date to Start	Check Progress
Ex. Cut out sweets after 8pm.	December 1st	March 1st

Final test. On a scale of 1 to 10, how confident are you that you will make the change?

not at all confident   never been more ready
1   2   3   4   5   6   7   8   9   10

What will it take to move your confidence to a 10? Identify specific chapters you need to go back to and/or focus areas we've covered you need to give more attention to.

Ex. Address my fear of inadequacy/feeling like I am unworthy of a better life. need to reread Chapter 13.

_____

_____

Ready, Set, Courage!

Visit therequisitecourage.com/bonusmaterials to download your fully integrated guide to putting courage in action complete with bonus activities.

Conclusion

Perhaps you're expecting me to welcome you to the final stage of courage. The finish line. The other side. The side of life where you are never afraid, never unsure, and always courageous. That would be great, if only it were possible.

Instead, let me welcome you to the *Under Construction* portion of your life.

You now see the cyclical nature of courage. When you learn to harness the power of fear and build a life that wholeheartedly reflects your values, you will see misalignment and inauthenticity as challenges to overcome. The fight isn't over until someone gets knocked out. If you keep getting up after falling, a champion is never crowned.

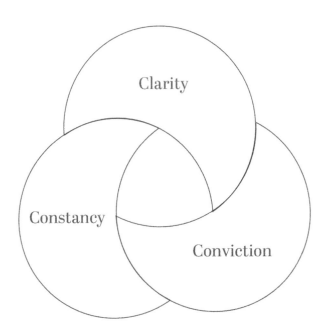

Continue to clarify who you are and what you stand for; find and hold conviction over your purpose; establish daily practices that breed resolve and build resilience. These elements of courage are interconnected. Your path to courage may ebb and flow between them as the tenets of the requisite courage rely upon another for application and effectiveness.

~~~~

Remember my coworker and long-time friend, Michelle? Well, she was right all those years ago. I haven't failed because I've never stopped. When the jigsaw puzzle isn't coming together, I keep at it. When I stop finding fulfillment in crafting the perfect resume story, I reassess and take the business in a new direction. When I invest in a fifteen-thousand-dollar webinar series that flops in the market, I refocus energy into another product line. When I expand the business and we are hit by a pandemic nearly shutting us down four weeks later, I pivot. When I want to test my own courage theory, I face my fears of failure, rejection, the unknown, isolation, inadequacy, and success and write a book about courage.

Life shrinks and expands in proportion to one's courage.
—Anaïs Nin

I learned the value of clarity, conviction, and constancy through my own personal brand. Growing the business around where my strengths are, means letting go of what doesn't work. It takes a lot to live with courage. Some fearless deeds are easier than others. But stepping through the fear and into the light we silence the ogres. Then we can inspire others through our greatest—and weakest—moments.

Courage is being afraid but going on anyhow. Courage is the power to let go of the familiar and step in that unknown, extending beyond what you once knew.

Life is full of circumstances that will bring you to your knees. The choice lies in whether you go down and stay down or pick yourself back up to face another day. There is a path through the valley of change and fear. *The Requisite Courage* is your guide.

Speeches, coaching, workshops, and program management

My vision is to inspire and equip millions of professionals to be courageous in their career and life. If you are looking to unleash your potential and that of your organization, I'd like to hear from you.

My years spent climbing the corporate ladder ignited a spark within to pave the way for living and working in alignment—

with authenticity and audacity. Collaboration with individual and corporate partners built the foundation for a systematic, evidence-based approach to career management that reduces turnover, increases productivity, and heightens employee engagement.

The best practices gleaned from my experiences are the lifeblood of services and tools I offer—services I hope you'll take advantage of to gain the skills and confidence you need for success. To get on my calendar, call 216-356-6561 or email me at kris@professionalcourage.com.

Acknowledgments

*At times our own light goes out and is rekindled
by a spark from another person. Each one of us has
cause to think deep gratitude of those who have
lighted the flame within us.*
—Albert Schweitzer

Rick. Thank you for being everything I ever needed. You remain true to our vows, supplying boundless love and encouragement. Your intellect and generosity inspire and enhance our family in new ways each day. Through good times and bad, you have loved deeply and allowed me to become the very best version of myself. I love you, Richard William McGuigan. I am forever grateful that the universe brought you to me in those skinny jeans.

Claire. You gave me fight. Your entry into the world sparked a fire that pushes me to always do better and strive to be the role model you deserve. The beauty of your heart and the power of your mind make you unstoppable. You have all the courage you will ever need inside of you. Never doubt that.

Matt. Your love and compassion and strength have impact far greater than you realize. You bring sunshine into my life with countless small yet significant gestures—a sweet smile, a reassuring glance, an encouraging "You do you, Momma." Watching you become your own man while embodying the best parts of Ricky is my greatest joy

Leanne Wadenpfuhl. You are undoubtedly the driving force behind this body of work. You created accountability, continuity, and a safe space to explore ideas and fears. Your brilliance contributed to this book and my life in ways that I cannot even begin to describe. Thank you for believing with me and in me. I never realized what a game changer that inflatable slide would be.

Mom. You are a force to be reckoned with. Your open mind and sense of self taught me to be strong and proud and capable. Thank you for being constant. Thank you for nurturing my independence. We both know why you didn't live in my back pocket growing up, but I sure like having you beside me now.

Dad. Whether seated next me in the truck or shouting from the crowd, you have been there all along. Cheering me on. Believing in me. As I raise my own family, I am acutely aware of the support and encouragement you provide. I can hear it loud and clear. And I am so grateful.

Grandma Judy and Papa Chuck. Your thoughts and hearts were with me throughout this process. I will forever be in awe and impacted by how readily you opened your homes and hearts to us. You are deeply missed.

Kathy. Since the very beginning, you always found your own way to love and support me. From blobs to quilts, adolescent advice to adult pep talks, named toothbrushes to social media posts, you never fail to boost me up. Thank you for being my perpetual cheerleader.

Christine, James, Jason, and Shola. The collective wisdom, inspiration, and support within our mastermind is almost unspeakable. Thank you for welcoming me into such a formidable group.

Kim Avery. You have given me so much. Your coaching has been life changing. Thank you for consistently finding just the right questions to get me out of my own way. Thank you for making me a better coach and a better person. Thank you for giving me professional courage.

Christine. The best kind of people are the ones that believe in you so much, you start to believe in you too. You are my best person.

Annie. You have given me a literal lifetime of love and laughter and I cannot imagine anyone I would rather cackle with into old age.

Karen. Times change, people change. Yet, your importance in my life has been a constant. From those very first moments with a rather talkative professor, you have stretched my mind to think far outside of its comfort zone.

Elaine. We crossed paths in life too late in life, but it was surely fate that brought us together. I am better for having met you—a beautiful reminder that God knows just what She is doing.

Stephanie. Remember that it takes a strong woman to know one. You are braver than you realize. Your talent, beauty, courage, and heart are to be admired.

Michelle. Your friendship has been one of my greatest blessings. I am so grateful you have allowed me to share in your celebrations and obstacles/trials/tests through the years. Thank you for the nudge.

Jen. In my darkest moment, you patiently waited for me to turn on the light. Thank you for believing in me when it mattered most.

Jessica. You are my favorite person to raise a glass with. Thank you for always being there to celebrate the big moments. Lou, just become a member already.

Rita. You embody courage and determination and give off a glow that brightens the path for all those who have the pleasure of knowing you. Thank you for proving that true friendship knows no distance or time.

Phyllis. Your smile radiates a warmth and kindness that is palpable. Thank you for sharing your beauty with me.

To the friends and family that inspire and challenge me to live courageously, thank you for being part of my journey.

To my clients who have given me the privilege of serving you and allowing me to be witness to your courage, thank you for the honor.

To my book review crew, thank you for your generosity, commitment, and thoughtful feedback. Your time and talents helped shape my thoughts and ideas into something worthy of publication.

To David Hancock and the entire family at Morgan James Publishing, thank you for making this dream a reality.

About the Author

Kris McGuigan is a Board Certified Coach and career strategist who has helped countless people step up and stand out in the marketplace. A featured speaker at Fortune 500 companies, small business associations, industry conferences, and globally broadcast summits, Kris uses her own story to guide clients and audiences to success in an ever-changing job mar-  ket. She resides in Broadview Heights, Ohio with her husband Rick, their two children Claire and Matthew, and a mini golden named Geoffrey.

Reading Group Guide

All individuals can access the courage required to demonstrate bravery in their personal and professional lives. By rigorously pursuing the exercises outlined in Courage in Action, readers will automatically set in motion a process to spark change in their lives.

Consider collaborating with other courage seekers as you digest the concepts presented in this book. As we know from our conversation on interpersonal support, a defined cohort of collaborators can offer a platform for knowledge sharing and a safe space for vulnerability about challenges and struggles. The questions below will support group discussions for application and heightened comprehension.

Discussion Questions:

1. What prompted you to read *The Requisite Courage*? Did the book inspire you to pursue courage in a way you had not previously thought of?

2. In Chapter 1, McGuigan says, "If you're living life, you've experienced change." What types of external and self-inflicted change have you experienced in your own life? Do you think most people gravitate towards voluntary change? Why or why not?

3. McGuigan identifies five fears that impact our response to change and pursuit of courageous action. In general, which of these fears do you think is most common? Which

fear might be hardest for people to acknowledge and face? Were you surprised by your own quiz results at the end of Chapter 3?

4. One of the ways McGuigan explores clarity is through self-discovery and the identification of core values. Do you think most people are aware of how value identification impacts their everyday lives? Why or why not?

5. If we are able to articulate what we want in life, why is bringing it to bear so difficult? Why are we hesitant to put forth the effort to implement change in our lives? What advice does McGuigan offer for strengthening your conviction?

6. McGuigan uses vulnerable stories of her own life to illustrate each of the three C's. Did any of these personal stories in particular strike a chord with you? Explain why.

7. McGuigan cites the Four Pillars of Constancy: doing above thinking, manageable above monumental, pausing above pushing, and support above setbacks. Which one of the four pillars resonates the most with you, and why?

8. In Chapter 16, McGuigan advises that, "You don't need to sit back and wait for the universe to work in your favor. You have the power to beckon its abundance." What do you think of this premise?

9. The concept of perpetual beta as a means of granting permission for imperfection is introduced in Chapter 18. What strategies for putting this framework into practice does McGuigan outline?

10. Have you put into practice all of the Courage in Action exercises? What have you learned from putting these techniques into action in your personal or professional life? Which assignment have you found most to be the most

challenging for you? Which assignment has had the most positive impact and why?

11. McGuigan offers readers multiple methods to train your brain to achieve a growth mindset: activating event diagram, the frequency illusion, powerful questions, and focusing on what matters. Which concept do you believe will be the most helpful for you to maintain a growth mindset during the challenging times? Why?

12. McGuigan says "Our commitment to our purpose is displayed most prominently in times of chaos." What do you think of this statement?

Endnotes

1 Vishwas Chavan, *VishwaSutras: Universal Principles for Living: Inspired by Real-Life Experiences*, (Author House UK, 2012).

2 Nirmita Panchal et al., "The Implications of COVID-19 for Mental Health and Substance Use," KFF, February 10, 2021, kff.org/coronavirus-covid-19/issue-brief/the-implications-of-covid-19-for-mental-health-and-substance-use/

3 Maddy Savage, "Coronavirus: The possible long-term mental health impacts," (October 28, 2020), https://www.bbc.com/worklife/article/20201021-coronavirus-the-possible-long-term-mental-health-impacts

4 "Well Being Trust & The Robert Graham Center Analysis: The COVID Pandemic Could Lead to 75,000 Additional Deaths from Alcohol and Drug Misuse and Suicide," *Well Being Trust*, (May 2020), https://wellbeingtrust.org/areas-of-focus/policy-and-advocacy/reports/projected-deaths-of-despair-during-covid-19/

5 "About Cesar," Cesar Millan, accessed November 24, 2021, https://www.cesarsway.com/about-cesar/

6 Lindsay Dodgson, "Why we are bad at dealing with change—and 5 ways you can improve," (October 13, 2018), https://www.businessinsider.com/5-ways-to-help-you-deal-with-change-2018-10

7   Andrea Nagy Smith, "What Was Polaroid Thinking?" *Yale Insights*, (November 4, 2009), https://insights.som.yale.edu/insights/what-was-polaroid-thinking

8   Peter Gahan & Lakmal Abeysekera, "What shapes an individual's work values? An integrated model of the relationship between work values, national culture and self-construal," *The International Journal of Human Resource Management*, (January 26, 2009), 20:1, 126-147, https://doi.org/10.1080/09585190802528524

9   Rochi Zalani, "Screen Time Statistics 2021: Your Smartphone Is Hurting You," *Elite Content Marketer*, (November 5, 2021), https://elitecontentmarketer.com/screen-time-statistics/

10   Loes Meeussen and Colette Van Laar, "Feeling Pressure to Be a Perfect Mother Relates to Parental Burnout and Career Ambitions," *Frontiers in Psychology* 9:2113, (November 5, 2018), doi: 10.3389/fpsyg.2018.02113

11   Patrick Henz, "Failure is not an option," ethics playground blog, (August 26, 2015), https://ethicsplayground.wordpress.com/2015/08/26/failure-is-not-an-option/

12   "Alice Walker Biography," Biography.com, (last update May 6, 2021), https://www.biography.com/writer/alice-walker

13   Lauren Hoffman, "How Humans of New York Became Brandon Stanton's Full-Time Job," *CreativeLive*, (August 24, 2016), https://www.creativelive.com/blog/humans-new-york-brandon-stanton/

14   Aidy Bryant, interview by Willie Geist, *Sunday Sitdown with Willie Geist*, Simplecast, (January 19, 2020), https://sunday-sitdown-with-willie-geist.simplecast.com/episodes/aidy-bryant-2Q_hmTv_

15   Nesta McGregor, "LGBT+ History Month: NFL player Ryan Russell on his decision to come out as bisexual," *BBC*

Sport, (February 18, 2021), https://www.bbc.com/sport/american-football/56100701

16 Lola Fadulu, "Not Everyone Can Afford a Job They Love," *The Atlantic*, (July 17, 2018), https://www.theatlantic.com/technology/archive/2018/07/reshma-saujani-girls-who-code/562055/

17 Brian O'Keefe, "The smartest futurist on Earth," *Fortune Magazine*, (May 2, 2007), https://money.cnn.com/2007/05/01/magazines/fortune/kurzweil.fortune/index.htm

18 University of Exeter, "The Change Curve," PDF file, https://www.exeter.ac.uk/media/universityofexeter/humanresources/documents/learningdevelopment/the_change_curve.pdf

19 Wilt, Joshua A et al., "Authenticity and inauthenticity in narrative identity." *Heliyon* vol. 5,7 e02178. (July 31 2019), doi:10.1016/j.heliyon.2019.e02178

20 "MBTI Facts," The Myers-Briggs Company, (accessed November 24, 2021), https://www.themyersbriggs.com/en-US/Support/MBTI-Facts

21 "History of DiSC," DiSC Profile, (accessed November 24, 2021), https://www.discprofile.com/what-is-disc/history-of-disc

22 "About Keirsey Assessments," Keirsey, (accessed November 23, 2021), https://keirsey.com/assessments/about/

23 "How the Enneagram System Works," The Enneagram Institute, (accessed November 23, 2021), https://www.enneagraminstitute.com/how-the-enneagram-system-works

24 Morgan Smith, "The No. 1 habit successful leaders share, according to executive coaches who have worked with Apple and Twitter," *CNBC Make It*, (November 10, 2021), https://www.cnbc.com/2021/11/09/the-no-1-habit-successful-leaders-share-according-to-career-coaches.html

25   John Steinbeck, *East of Eden*, (New York: Penguin Classics; Reprint edition October 18, 2016)

26   Alex Wood, P. Linley, John Maltby, Michael Baliousis, and Stephen Joseph, "The Authentic Personality: A Theoretical and Empirical Conceptualization and the Development of the Authenticity Scale," *Journal of Counseling Psychology* Vol 55, (July 2008): 385-399

27   Aliya Alimujiang MPH, Ashley Wiensch, MPH, Jonathan Boss, MS, et al., "Association Between Life Purpose and Mortality Among US Adults Older Than 50 Years," *Journal of the American Medical Association,* (May 24, 2019), doi:10.1001/jamanetworkopen.2019.4270

28   Simon Sinek, *Start with Why* (New York: Portfolio; Illustrated edition December 27, 2011)

29   Erica Volini et al., "The worker-employer relationship disrupted," *Deloitte Insights,* (July 21, 2021), https://www2.deloitte.com/us/en/insights/focus/human-capital-trends/2021/the-evolving-employer-employee-relationship.html

30   Jacobus Gideon (Kobus) Maree, "Innovating Counseling for Self- and Career Construction: Theoretical Premises, Antecedents, and Associations." *Innovating Counseling for Self- and Career Construction: Connecting Conscious Knowledge with Subconscious Insight* (Switzerland: Springer 2020), doi:10.1007/978-3-030-48648-8_2

31   Michael E. Bratman, *Planning, Time, and Self-Governance: Essays in Practical Rationality*, (New York: Oxford University Press, July 2, 2018)

32   E. J. Masicampo and Roy F. Baumeister, "Consider it done! Plan making can eliminate the cognitive effects of unfulfilled goals," *Journal of Personality and Social Psychology*, (October 2011), doi: 10.1037/a0024192. PMID: 21688924

33   Pauline Rose Clance, and Suzanne A. Imes, "The Impostor Phenomenon in High Achieving Women: Dynamics and Therapeutic Interventions," *Psychotherapy: Theory Research and Practice*, 15, (1978) 241 247. http://www.paulineroseclance.com/pdf/ip_high_achieving_women.pdf

34   Carol Dweck, "The power of believing that you can improve," filmed November 2014 at TEDxNorrkoping, video, https://www.ted.com/talks/carol_dweck_the_power_of_believing_that_you_can_improve

35   Barbara Markway and Celia Ampel, *The Self-Confidence Workbook: A Guide to Overcoming Self-Doubt and Improving Self-Esteem*, (California: Althea Press; Workbook edition October 23, 2018)

36   A. Ellis, & R. M. Grieger, (Eds.). *Handbook of rational-emotive therapy*, Vol. 2. (1986), New York: Springer Publishing Company, https://psycnet.apa.org/record/1986-98458-000

37   Richard C. Mohs, "How Human Memory Works," HowStuffWorks.com,   (May 8 2007), https://science.howstuffworks.com/life/inside-the-mind/human-brain/human-memory.htm

38   Anina Rich, "What is the Baader-Meinhof Phenomenon?" *The LightHouse Macquaire University*, (July 22, 2020), https://lighthouse.mq.edu.au/article/july-2020/What-is-the-Baader-Meinhof-Phenomenon

39   David Hoffeld, "Want To Know What Your Brain Does When It Hears A Question?" *Fast Company*, (February 21, 2017),   https://www.fastcompany.com/3068341/want-to-know-what-your-brain-does-when-it-hears-a-question

40   Aimee Groth, "19 Amazing Ways CEO Howard Schultz Saved Starbucks," *Business Insider*, (June 19, 2011),

https://www.businessinsider.com/howard-schultz-turned-starbucks-around-2011-6

41 Daniel Goleman, *Focus: The Hidden Driver of Excellence*, (New York: Harper; Illustrated edition October 8, 2013)

42 Grant Cardone, *The 10X Rule: The Only Difference Between Success and Failure*, (New Jersey: Wiley; 1st edition April 26, 2011)

43 "Social Media Fact Sheet," *Pew Research Center*, (April 7, 2021), https://www.pewresearch.org/internet/fact-sheet/social-media/

44 Amy L Gonzales and Jeffrey T Hancock, "Mirror, Mirror on my Facebook Wall: Effects of Exposure to Facebook on Self-Esteem." *Cyberpsychology, Behavior and Social Networking* vol. 14,1-2 (2011): 79-83. doi:10.1089/cyber.2009.0411

45 Mel Robbins, *The 5 Second Rule: Transform your Life, Work, and Confidence with Everyday Courage*, (New York: Savio Republic; Illustrated edition February 28, 2017)

46 Stephen Hawking Biography. https://www.hawking.org.uk/biography

47 Tremayne, David, "Soichiro Honda: The man behind a legend," Grandprix.com, archived from the original, October 15, 2013) https://web.archive.org/web/20131015070520/http://www.grandprix.com/ft/ftdt017.html

48 Graham Hill, "She lost her arm in a shark attack, but surfer Bethany Hamilton is living 'an unstoppable life,'" *CNN Sports*, (October 25, 2019) https://www.cnn.com/2019/10/25/sport/bethany-hamilton-surfing-spt-intl/index.html

49 Stephen Covey, *The 7 Habits of Highly Effective People*, (New York: Simon & Schuster; 4th edition, May 19, 2020)

50   "History of Harley-Davidson," Las Vegas Harley-Davidson, (January 25, 2019), https://www.lasvegasharleydavidson. com/history-of-harley-davidson/

51   Malcolm Gladwell, *Outliers: The Story of Success*. (New York: Bay Back Books, June 1, 2011)

52   Joe Navarro, international bestselling author and body language expert. https://www.jnforensics.com/

53   Amy J. C. Cuddy, S. Jack Schultz, and Nathan E. Fosse, "P-Curving a More Comprehensive Body of Research on Postural Feedback Reveals Clear Evidential Value for Power-Posing Effects: Reply to Simmons and Simonsohn (2017)," *The ANNALS of the American Academy of Political and Social Science* 29, no. 4 (April 2018): 230–43. https://pubmed. ncbi.nlm.nih.gov/29498906/

54   Andy Molinsky, "Angela Duckworth Speaks on Grit and Her Early Career," *Psychology Today*, (June 2, 2019), https:// www.psychologytoday.com/us/blog/adaptation/201906/ angela-duckworth-speaks-grit-and-her-early-career

55   George S. Everly, Jr., "Building a Resilient Organizational Culture," *Harvard Business Review*, (June 24, 2011), https:// hbr.org/2011/06/building-a-resilient-organizat

56   A. McKee, R. Boyatzis & F. Johnston, *Becoming a resonant leader: Develop your emotional intelligence, renew your relationships, sustain your effectiveness*, (Boston: Harvard Business Review Press, 2008).

57   Daniel Isenberg, "The Tactics of Strategic Opportunism," *Harvard Business Review*, (March 1987). https://hbr. org/1987/03/the-tactics-of-strategic-opportunism

A free ebook edition is available with the purchase of this book.

To claim your free ebook edition:

1. Visit MorganJamesBOGO.com
2. Sign your name CLEARLY in the space
3. Complete the form and submit a photo of the entire copyright page
4. You or your friend can download the ebook to your preferred device

Morgan James
BOGO™

A **FREE** ebook edition is available for you or a friend with the purchase of this print book.

CLEARLY SIGN YOUR NAME ABOVE

Instructions to claim your free ebook edition:
1. Visit MorganJamesBOGO.com
2. Sign your name CLEARLY in the space above
3. Complete the form and submit a photo of this entire page
4. You or your friend can download the ebook to your preferred device

Print & Digital Together Forever.

Snap a photo

Free ebook

Read anywhere

Printed in the USA
CPSIA information can be obtained
at www.ICGtesting.com
LVHW021803090524
779310LV00004B/12

9 781631 958878